Clyde Belew

BY HENRY VAN DYKE

The Valley of Vision
Fighting for Peace
The Unknown Quantity
The Ruling Passion
The Blue Flower

Camp-Fires and Guide-Posts
Out-of-Doors in the Holy Land
Days Off
Little Rivers
Fisherman's Luck

Poems, Collection in one volume

Golden Stars
The Red Flower
The Grand Canyon, and Other Poems
The White Bees, and Other Poems
The Builders, and Other Poems
Music, and Other Poems
The Toiling of Felix, and Other Poems
The House of Rimmon

Studies in Tennyson
Poems of Tennyson

CHARLES SCRIBNER'S SONS

CAMP-FIRES
AND GUIDE-POSTS

From a photograph by Mathilde Weil.

The bird-bath in the garden.

CAMP-FIRES AND GUIDE-POSTS

A BOOK OF
ESSAYS AND EXCURSIONS

BY
HENRY VAN DYKE

*"When Paradise was lost I thought everything was ended.
But it was only begun."*
—SOLOMON SINGLEWITZ: *The Life of Adam.*

NEW YORK
CHARLES SCRIBNER'S SONS
1921

Copyright, 1920, 1921, by Charles Scribner's Sons

Published April, 1921

THE SCRIBNER PRESS

TO

MY DAUGHTER AND CHUM
PAULA VAN DYKE CHAPIN
OTHERWISE CALLED
LITTLE FUJI-SAN

PREFACE

Some of the chapters in this book were written as a series of monthly papers in *Scribner's Magazine* in the years 1920–21. I have ventured to add a few things,—interludes, you may call them,—which may be taken as talks by the camp-fire. At the end I have included four little chapters of remembrance,—*memoriæ posita*,—tributes to four beloved fellow-travellers.

HENRY VAN DYKE.

AVALON, February 22, 1921.

CONTENTS

		PAGE
I.	Camp-Fires and Guide-Posts	3
II.	A Certain Insularity of Islanders	19
III.	A Basket of Chips	37
IV.	Self, Neighbor, and Company	41
V.	Sympathetic Antipathies	59
VI.	Publicomania	77
VII.	Moving Day	83
VIII.	Firelight Views	100
IX.	Fishing in Strange Waters	120
X.	The Pathless Profession	142
XI.	A Mid-Pacific Pageant	152
XII.	Japonica	174
XIII.	Interludes on the Koto	198
XIV.	Suicidal Tendencies in Democracy	203
XV.	A Bundle of Letters	228
XVI.	Christmas Greens	233
XVII.	On Saying Good-Bye	251

CONTENTS

FELLOW-TRAVELLERS:

		PAGE
XVIII.	*An Old-Style American*	271
XIX.	*Interpreter's House*	290
XX.	*The Healing Gift*	300
XXI.	*A Traveller from Altruria*	310

ILLUSTRATIONS

The bird-bath in the garden	*Frontispiece*
	Facing page
The round stone tower	20
Is not moving day marked in all our calendars?	96
In andirons I would admit a little fancy	106
The ancient, apostolic, consolatory art of angling	140
A house with broad lanai *and long* pergola	160
The temple-garden where the iris blooms around the pond	188
Camp-fires beneath the trees	262

CAMP-FIRES AND GUIDE-POSTS

I

CAMP-FIRES AND GUIDE-POSTS

THE title of these rambling essays is taken from two things that are pleasant and useful on the common ways of life.

Let me confess at the outset that by camp-fires and guide-posts I intend more than the literal meaning of the words. I use them for their significance.

The camp-fire is the conservative symbol. It invites to rest and fellowship and friendly council, not unmixed with that good cheer which is suggested when we call a conference of wits a "symposium." There is no denying the fact that man's best discourse has always been at a common meal, whether spread on the green grass or on a mahogany table. Of the elders of Israel in the Exodus, it is recorded that "they saw God and did eat and drink." This is a gentle hint that however soulful a man's soul may be, in his present mixed estate the body had its claims, which it is both lawful and necessary to satisfy, in order that the spiritual part may not be hampered and disordered. Hunger, thirst, and indigestion are unfavorable alike to clear thought and calm devotion.

The guide-post is the progressive sign. It calls us to continue our journey, and gives information in regard to direction and distance, which (if correct) has considerable value to the traveller.

Every social theory, every moral maxim, every appeal of preacher or political orator, every bit of propaganda printed or spoken, yes, even every advertisement in the newspapers or on the billboards, whether false or true, is of the nature of a guide-post.

Every place where men rest and repose with warmth to cheer them—the hollow in the woods where pilgrims or tramps gather about the blazing sticks, the snug cottage where the kettle simmers on the hearth, the royal castle where an ancient coat-of-arms is carved on the mantelpiece, the vast palatial hotel where sovereign democracy flaunts its new-found wealth and commercial travellers bask in the heat of concealed steam-radiators—every one of these is nothing more nor less than a camp-fire.

No human progress is unbroken and continuous. No human resting-place is permanent. Where are

AND GUIDE-POSTS

Pharaoh's Palace, and Solomon's Temple, and the House of Cæsar, and Cicero's Tusculum, and Horace's Sabine farm?

I remember what General William Tecumseh Sherman—fine old campaigner—said to me when he first came to New York to live in his own house. "I've made a new camp. Plenty of wood and water. Come over."

We might get more comfort out of this sane and wholesome philosophy of life, if it were not for the violent extremists of the Right and the Left, who revile and buffet us alternately when we try to push ahead and when we stop to think. I have good friends on both sides, but at times they treat me vilely as an enemy.

The trouble with the Radicals is that they are always urging us to travel somewhither, anywhither, ignoring the past, condemning the present, and hurling ourselves blindfold into the future.

The trouble with the Conservatives is that they are always lulling us to stay where we are, to be content with our present comforts, and to look with optimistic eyes on the bright side of our neighbors' discomforts.

Neither pessimism nor optimism pleases me. I

am a meliorist,—to use the word which Doctor John Brown of Edinburgh coined in 1858.

Therefore I refuse to engage in the metaphysical triangular conflict between the past, the present, and the future. It means nothing to me. Yesterday is a memory. To-morrow is a hope. To-day is the fact. But tell me, would the fact be what it is without the memory and the hope? Are not all three equally real?

I grant you there is a distinction between the actual and the imaginary. But it is not a difference in essence. It is only a difference in origin and form. What we call the actual has its origin in a fact outside of us. What we call the imaginary has its origin in a fact within us.

A burned finger and a burning indignation are equally real.

Memory is simply imagination looking back: hope, looking forward.

The imaginary is not non-existent. It exists in the mind—the very same place where every perception through the senses has its present and only being.

When I was a boy I cut my hand with my first pocket-knife. But the physical scar of that actual

AND GUIDE-POSTS

accident, now almost invisible, is less vivid than the memory of the failure of my ambition to become a great orator. In that collegiate contest, fifty years ago, the well-prepared phrase fled from my paralyzed brain,

"*vox faucibus haesit*,"

and I sat down feeling that life was ended. But it was not.

You remember, as of yesterday, those pleasant afternoon walks on Fifth Avenue from Madison Square to Central Park, in the last quarter of the Nineteenth Century, when the air was clean and bright, the sky-line low, and on every block you had greetings from good friends. To-day, if duty compels, you plunge through that same mile-and-a-half, shut in by man-made cliffs of varying degrees of ugliness, stifled by fumes of gasolene from the conglomerate motor-cars, and worming your way through malodorous or highly perfumed throngs of "Parthians, Medes, and Elamites, dwellers in Mesopotamia and Judæa, Cappadocia, Pontus, and Asia, Phrygia, Pamphylia, Egypt, and strangers of Rome, Jews and proselytes, Cretes and Arabians." Few indeed are the native Americans you meet, struggling like yourself among the conflicting tides,—

"rari nantes in gurgite vasto."

Yet, even on such a walk, if you think serenely, you have a hope of something better in the long to-morrow: a modern city in which the curse of crowding shall be mitigated by wiser dispositions of traffic, transportation, and housing: a city in which there shall be room for homes and playgrounds, as well as for temples and court-houses: a city in which the rights of property shall be safeguarded chiefly as essential to the supreme right of life.

The memory, the fact, the hope, are equally real. But tell me, brother, can we really make sure of our guide-posts unless we take counsel together beside our camp-fires?

The secret of perpetual motion has not yet been discovered. Human nature demands intervals of rest and relaxation as the unexempt condition of our mortal frailty.

Here is where I find my stance for a drive. Go forward we must, unless we are willing to slip backward. But we cannot know that we are going for-

AND GUIDE-POSTS

ward, without stopping to talk over our common concerns beside the camp-fire.

Good humor is one of the prerequisites of sound judgment.

I have seen needful work done by men in excitement and an ill temper, but never truth discovered nor creative things accomplished. My old gardener used to swear horribly when he was rooting out poison-ivy. But when he was studying how to make flowers or vegetables grow better, he was in a friendly mood—whistling or singing.

Emerson has a good word on this. "Nothing will supply the want of sunshine to peaches, and to make knowledge valuable, you must have the cheerfulness of wisdom. Whenever you are sincerely pleased you are nourished. The joy of the spirit indicates its strength. All healthy things are sweet-tempered. Genius works in sport, and goodness smiles to the last; and, for the reason, that whoever sees the law which distributes things does not despond, but is animated by great desires and endeavors. He who desponds betrays that he has not seen it."

But what about the man who frets and fumes and froths at the mouth when he propounds his

CAMP-FIRES

favorite dogma? What about the guide-post enthusiasts who pronounce double damnation on us if we do not rush forward at once on their favorite roads to Utopia? What about the camp-fire sedentaries who declare that unless we "stand pat" precisely where we are, we are doomed to perdition?

Methinks, gentlemen, you do protest too much. The violence of your protest indicates a certain insecurity of the ground whereon you stand. You would base your programme upon ignorance of what men learned in Athens, Sparta, Carthage, Sicily, and Rome, long ago. That will not go! We fall back upon one of those vital phrases with which slang has enriched our language—"*show me!*"

Nor are we willing, if we can prevent it, to have tried upon our tender bodies and souls the old experiments which were tried so long ago and which resulted in lamentable failure.

Why suffer twice to learn the same lesson?

Communism, agrarianism, proletarianism, anarchism, have all had their day, and it was a bad day,— in Athens and Sparta and Rome and Jerusalem and Paris. Why give them another day?

The divine right of kings and capitalists to impose their will upon their fellow men has been tested

AND GUIDE-POSTS

many times and has always failed to make good before the throne of Eternal Wisdom and Righteousness. The bloody bankruptcy of the French reign of terror was no worse, and no better, than the breakdown of the attempt of the Holy Alliance to re-establish the tyranny of hereditary titles and unjust prerogatives.

Why ask us to return to these old discredited theories? They are not really guide-posts. They are signs of "no thoroughfare." Give us something really new, gentlemen. Think out some better way of co-operation between the "haves" and the "have-nots." Devise some better mode of inducing the lazy to work, and of restraining the clever and industrious from claiming exorbitant gains. That is what we need, as surely as two and two make four.

If you can do this, I promise you that a considerable company of the intellectual middle class, neither "high-brows" who think they know it all, nor "low-brows" who maintain that nothing is worth knowing, will be ready for a promising adventure. Meantime we follow the old guide-posts which have been proved, and take our needful ease by the camp-fires where we find creature comforts

CAMP-FIRES

and friendly talk. And if our camp is attacked by brigands, we shall be ready for them.

I was rereading the other day one of the dialogues of Plato, called *Theætetus*, and came upon a passage which seemed to depict the position of thoughtful people in our own time. Plato is speaking of a philosopher endeavoring to instruct and guide a practical man of the world. "But, O my friend," says he, "when he draws the other into the upper air, and gets him out of his pleas and rejoinders into the contemplation of justice and injustice in their own nature, or from the commonplaces about the happiness of kings to the consideration of government, and of human happiness and misery in general—what they are and how a man should seek after the one and avoid the other—when that narrow, keen, little legal mind of his is called to account about all this, he gives the philosopher his revenge. For being dizzied by the height at which he is hanging, he being dismayed and lost and stammering out broken words, is laughed at not only by Thracian handmaidens or any other uneducated persons, for they have no eye for the situation, but by every man who has not been brought up a slave. Such are the two

AND GUIDE-POSTS

characters, Theodorus; the one of the philosopher or gentleman, who may be excused for appearing futile and inefficient when he has to perform some servile office, such as packing a bag, or flavoring a sauce, or making a flattering speech; the other, of the man of affairs who is able to do every service smartly and neatly, but knows not how to wear his cloak like a gentleman; still less does he acquire the music of speech or hymn, in the true life which is lived by immortals or men blessed by heaven."

This is a fair description, two thousand years old, of the difference between the "high-brow" and the "low-brow." But from this Plato goes on to tell us something more important. "Evils," says he, "can never perish; for there must always remain something which is antagonistic to good. . . . But, O my friend, you cannot easily convince mankind that they should avoid vice or pursue virtue for the reason which the majority give, in order, forsooth, to appear respectable;—this is what people are always repeating, and this, in my judgment, is an old wives' tale. Let us get back to the truth! In God is no unrighteousness at all— He is altogether righteous; and there is nothing more like Him than the man among us who is the most righteous. And the true wisdom of men, and their nothingness and cowardice, are closely bound up with this. For to know this is true wisdom and manhood, and to ignore this is folly and vice. All other kinds of so-called wisdom, such as the wisdom of politicians or the wisdom of the arts, are coarse and vulgar. The unrighteous man, or the sayer and doer of unholy things, had far better not cherish the illusion that his roguery is cleverness. Let us tell him frankly that he does not realize what kind of creature he is. He does not know the penalty of unrighteousness: not stripes and death, as he supposes, which evil-doers often elude, but a final punishment from which there is no escape."

You would not take so long and stern a sermon from a modern preacher. But will you not consider it from the broad-shouldered, wide-browed Plato, who lived four hundred years before Christ? Will you not read it as a comment upon those modern knaves who twist the guide-posts around and swear that good is evil and vice is virtuous; those long-haired, lantern-jawed mockers who protest that property is theft and that highway robbery is the triumph of justice?

I do not mean to be drawn into a discussion of

AND GUIDE-POSTS

the bold brutalities of the Bolsheviki in Russia, or the sneaking villainies of the I. W. W. in America. These lie outside of the region of literature. They are to be met not with essays and orations, but with laws and guns. The decencies of life, the securities of home, the safeguards of social order, having been won, by toil and fighting, from the abyss of barbarism, will not be suffered to perish. Neither the fury of the antisocial maniacs, nor the sentimentalism of the social imbeciles will be permitted to destroy them. We look to statesmen and warriors to take care of this.

But what I am thinking of is the normal life of humanity—a journey with frequent, necessary halts—as Matthew Arnold describes it in *Rugby Chapel*:

> "See! In the rocks of the world
> Marches the host of mankind,
> A feeble, wavering line.
> Where are they tending? A god
> Marshall'd them, gave them their goal.
> Ah, but the way is so long!
> Years they have been in the wild:
> Sore thirst plagues them, the rocks
> Rising all round overawe;
> Factions divide them, their host

Threatens to break, to dissolve.
—Ah, keep, keep them combined!
Else, of the myriads who fill
That army, not one shall arrive;
Sole shall they stray; in the rocks
Stagger forever in vain,
Die one by one in the waste."

Yes, we must hold together, and go forward together, and take our wayside rest together. That is what I mean to write about in these essays. The enjoyment of the camp-fires. The scrutiny of the guide-posts.

But you must not suspect me of having an ulterior design of springing a new theory of the universe upon you, nor of subtly advertising a panacea for all

"The heartache, and the thousand natural shocks
That flesh is heir to."

No, gentle reader, I am as much in the dark as you are, and with you I suffer

"The slings and arrows of outrageous fortune."

'Tis a rough, confused, turbulent age in which we have to live. But it is the only age that is given

AND GUIDE-POSTS

to us. Let us make the best of it. And above all let us not lose either our loyalty to truth or our sense of humor.

For my own part I confess my prepossession in favor of the small but useful virtues—like fair play, and punctuality, and common courtesy.

If I write of these things, more than of the ultimate ethical theories which engage our modern philosophists, you will understand and forgive me. I do not profess to have solved the riddle of existence. Let us try out our guesses together by the camp-fire.

And you, my young brother, don't think that because I am old, I am necessarily aged, and against you. You are my friend, my hope, my reliance.

I am not quite so sure of anything—not even of my doubts, denials, and prejudices—as I was in my youth. But I have had some experience of what agrees with body and soul, as Keats says in his ode to the bards of passion and mirth,

"What doth strengthen and what maim."

By that knowledge I try to steer my course toward peace and a certain degree of usefulness.

The minor morals of life attract me. I like real

and decent folk of all creeds and parties. But I have no confidence in catchwords, either of autocracy or democracy, nor in universal suffrage as the cure-all of man's infirmity.

Christ was crucified by a referendum.

II

A CERTAIN INSULARITY OF ISLANDERS

THIS curious quality of human nature first attracted my notice some forty years ago, when I went to work in Newport, an ancient little city (from the American point of view) situate on the island of Rhode Island, in the State of Rhode Island.

There, in the centre of Touro Park, stands the round stone tower which the romanticists revere as relic of the discovery of America by the Norsemen centuries before Columbus sailed, and which the factualists regard as the remains of a windmill built in the seventeenth century to grind Indian corn.

But you are mistaken if you suppose that a mere archæological dispute like this made any difference in the insular feeling of the native Newporters.

Was the tower built by Leif the Viking when he found his colony of Vinland? That only showed how well the old Norse adventurer "knew his way about," when he picked out the island of Rhode

Island as the most beautiful and salubrious spot in a whole new world,—an island abundant in the wild fox-grapes with which Nature fills her loving-cup for man, and blessed with a douce climate in which the Gulf Stream tempers alike the rigors of winter and the ardors of summer to an enjoyable though relaxing suavity.

Was the tower erected by a prudent and prosperous English colonist to triturate his maize in the days of Roger Williams? That only illustrated the well-known fact that the corn-meal of Rhode Island,—white, minutely granular, and highly nutritious,—was, and still is, the finest on earth, and positively the only cereal fit for the making of the succulent Johnny-cake, unexcelled among the foods of mankind.

I found the insularity of these islanders absolutely correct about the superiority of their corn-meal; also about the supremacy of the Rhode Island turkey as a "*pièce de résistance*" in a banquet.

But I found much more than this. Rhode Island was not, as I in my Knickerbocker ignorance had supposed, a fraction of New England, supine between Massachusetts and Connecticut. It was an independent and sovereign, though diminutive,

The round stone tower.

A CERTAIN INSULARITY

State. It had its own traditions and its own ideals, inherited from the Founder, Roger Williams, that best of Puritans,—who held that the freedom of his own conscience implied an equal liberty for others.

The magic names of Massachusetts,—Adams, Endicott, Quincy, Cabot, Lodge, Hallowell, Hancock, and so on,—carried no spell with them in Rhode Island. There Arnold, Greene, Coggeshall, Coddington, Clarke, Easton, Vernon, Buffum, Hammett, Sheffield, and so on,—forgive me if I forget a few,—were the names of insular renown. Their inheritors, no matter whether they were now engaged in commerce, carpentry, or agriculture, or living quietly on diminished estates in gambrel-roofed houses, belonged to the first families.

The old retired sea-captains,—portly, ruddy men, who had a trace of profanity in their speech even when they argued for the orthodox religion,—formed a class of their own. Like Ulysses they could say:

"Much have I seen and known: cities of men,
   And manners, climates, councils, governments."

But unlike that insatiable old wanderer, they preferred the climate of their own sea-girt isle to any other in the world. Its ways and manners, councils and traditions, contented them to the core. They had sailed abroad, come home to the best, and settled down. They were conserved conservatives.

This was the atmosphere and spirit of the old Newport, with its narrow streets, gambrel roofs, house-doors opening directly upon the sidewalk, square chimneys, and small-paned windows. The new Newport, which was at that time just beginning to expand its million-dollar "cottages" along the Cliffs, and to display its expensive and much-divorced social luxuriance along the misnamed Bellevue Avenue, made little impression on the real islanders. They regarded it mainly as a "passing show," and incidentally as an opportunity of increased gains from real estate and retail trade.

I recall an observation made by my father when he was walking with me and one of my Newport deacons on the Avenue. Gilded youths passed us in gorgeous equipages, and were pointed out and identified. That was so-and-so, or such-a-one, who had married this-or-the-other millionaire's daughter. "Well," said my governor, smiling under his brown beard, "I think this part of Newport ought to be called 'Son-in-Law City.'" The remark passed into a proverb in the old town

A CERTAIN INSULARITY

They were pleasant people to live and work with, those native Newporters and the folks who had settled in with them. Their self-content, not being bumptious, sweetened their ways and made them easy-going. Many friends I found among them: a gentle, lame bookseller, who knew both men and books; a schoolmaster whose latinity was as admirable as his natural wit; a cabinet-maker whose hand-wrought furniture was without a flaw; a shoemaker whose soles were as honest as his soul; a retired gentleman whose chief luxuries were good literature, good music, and good talk; and most of all, my predecessor in the pastorate, the old Domine, learned and humorous, a famous story-teller, whose favorite doctrine was that the first of the virtues is humility,—of which he had plenty and was very proud.

In fact the insularity of the place, as I grew to comprehend it, gave me sincere pleasure. The only point on which it irked me was that these island-people seemed to know little and care less about the distinguished position in American history of my own particular island,—Long Island, with its famous metropolis of Brooklyn, then a large New England village, which has since been absorbed into the cosmopolis of New York. This indifference to the claims of Brooklyn chafed me a bit; but I accepted it with the generous superiority of youth. So I had four happy years in Newport.

The next time I had occasion to consider the true meaning of insularity was when I began to make acquaintance with the island of Great Britain, including its local divisions of England, Scotland, and Wales. Here is a wonderful bit of "land surrounded by water," situate off the western coast of Europe, which has a more distinct individuality and has exercised a more powerful influence on the history of the modern world than any country of the continent.

Now what do you find in contact with the Briton, social, intellectual, political, as the basis of his thought and feeling? The conviction that his island is central and superior, and that his own way of looking at things and of doing things is the right way.

"Every Englishman," wrote Novalis in a spirit of German mockery, "is an island." Yes, beloved philosopher; but at least he is separate from the mainland of Prussia; and he regards the surrounding sea not merely as his protection, but also as his means of communication with the rest of the world.

A CERTAIN INSULARITY

He is the most widely travelled of provincials. But he never forgets where he came from.

The Englishman is that member of the human family who regards his personal habits as sacred rites. His morning tub accompanies him into Thibet. His afternoon tea is a function in India. His pale ale is placarded on the Pyramids.

The thing that an American notices on first meeting an Englishman, at home or abroad, is his high coast-line. If you pass that chalk cliff, you discover the richness, fertility, hospitality of the island. Nowhere do you feel more a foreigner (except for the language) than on your first arrival in England; and nowhere more at home, when you have lived through the early shocks into a friendly intimacy.

The notable social quality of England is the distinction between classes and the simplicity within them. George Washington would have understood this better than we do. But even now it is disappearing a little as the House of Lords is periodically enlarged from the ranks of brewers and makers of newspapers and of soap. All honors to them! But they are still expected to conform in manners, to say nothing of religion, if they wish to find their places in the blessed British insularity.

CAMP-FIRES

Often in England have I met with frankness, bluffness, even brusqueness; but only twice with rudeness. Once it was from a duchess of plebeian birth; which was not astonishing. The other time it was from a shrivelled curator in a university library; which gave me a shiver of surprise.

But since then, what courtesy and hospitality have I found in English and Scotch houses, and in the most ancient of British universities, gray home of the golden dream! What friendly and fruitful talk in mellow voices, cheered by sound wine before an open fire! What intimate understanding of the best meaning of culture! What sincere disregard of the pratings of publicity! What good fellowship, based on the ideals of fine literature and fair morals, shown in Chaucer, Shakespeare, Milton, and their followers!

The only difficulty I had was to persuade some of those modern Englishmen that the supposed Americanism, "I guess," was a direct inheritance from Spenser and Shakespeare; and that our pronunciation of "been" to rhyme with "bin," and our habit of saying "different from" instead of "different to" had good old English authority behind them. My friends were delightfully insular, but they did not

A CERTAIN INSULARITY

go far enough back in the history of their *insula*. Finally I gave up the effort to enlighten them and settled down comfortably with my "Americanisms."

I had many opportunities to observe the course of the American Rhodes Scholars in Oxford. It appeared to divide itself into three periods. First, *irritation*, when they rebelled against English customs. Second, *imitation*, when they vainly endeavored to acquire an Oxford accent and manner. Third (but this only for the finest of them), *assimilation*, when they took in the best of English culture and sweetened their inborn, inbred Americanism with it.

Emerson wrote in 1856: "I am afraid that English nature is so rank and aggressive as to be a little incompatible with any other. The world is not wide enough for two."

Hawthorne, a little later, wrote: "An American is not apt to love the English people as a whole, on whatever length of acquaintance. I fancy that they would value our regard, and even reciprocate it in their ungracious way, if we could give it to them in spite of all rebuffs; but they are beset by a curious and inevitable infelicity, which compels them, as it were, to keep up what they consider a wholesome bitterness of feeling between themselves and all other nationalities, especially that of America."

These were comments marked by asperity more than by urbanity. But it must be remembered that they were made about the period of our Civil War, which was not precisely the golden age of Anglo-American relations. I think the earlier remarks of Irving and the later observations of Lowell were more to the point.

The English took unfavorable criticisms from this side of the water ill, yet with far less perturbation and indignation than we Americans showed at the caustic caricatures of Mrs. Trollope and Charles Dickens. We knew that some of our people were rude and crude; but why remind us of it so rudely and crudely? We were furiously angry and we let the world know it. The English may have been equally vexed, but they made less fuss about it, perhaps because of their more perfect insularity.

The man whose good opinion of himself is solid can afford to be imperturbable. It is when vanity is insecure that it grows touchy.

Is not English the only great language in which the pronoun of the first person singular is capital-

A CERTAIN INSULARITY

ized? How monumentally imposing is that upper case "I"! If a writer is egoistic the capitals stretch across his page like a colonnade. When he writes "we," he descends to the lower case.

But this orthographic solipsism, mark you, is shared by Americans, Canadians, Australians, New Zealanders,—all who use the English tongue. It is therefore not to be set down to insularity, but to individualism,—a stark, ineradicable, valuable quality of these various folks whose thoughts and feelings have been nourished by the same language.

It comes to its philosophic climax in the Yankee Emerson who held the infinity and sufficiency of the private man, and declared, "I wish to say what I think and feel to-day, with the proviso that perhaps to-morrow I shall contradict it all." No Briton, not even Carlyle, could beat that.

It is all very well to have confidence in yourself, but when it passes into contempt for the rest of mankind it becomes a different matter. Plato said: "Self-will is a companion of solitude."

There are some men who consider comment on the faults of others equivalent to an exhibition of their own virtues. Self-complacency of that kind is seldom shared by the neighbors.

CAMP-FIRES

Once in a while a Briton, otherwise of good disposition and temperament, falls into that extravagance of insularity. Sidney Smith gave an illustration of it when he wrote in 1820, "Who reads an American book? or goes to an American play? or looks at an American picture or statue?"

Well, at that very time, a noted English poet, Thomas Campbell, had read the poems of Philip Freneau of New Jersey closely enough to steal a fine verse from one of them,—

"The hunter and the deer, a shade,"—

and embody it in his own poem *O'Connor's Child*. At that very time Lamb was praising the *Journal* of the American Quaker, John Woolman; and Walter Scott was admiring Washington Irving's *Sketch Book*. At that very time an American painter, Benjamin West of Philadelphia, was, and had been for twenty-seven years, president of the Royal Academy in London. Nay, it is reported that Sidney Smith himself jocosely threatened to disinherit his daughter if she did not like the writings of Benjamin Franklin. So you see his supercilious comment in the *Review* was of the nature of an aberration.

A CERTAIN INSULARITY

Something of the same nature I noted in Matthew Arnold, the apostle of sweetness and light, when he visited this country some thirty odd years ago. A genial Scotch-American in Brooklyn, a *bon-vivant* of the old school, made a feast for him, at which there was excellent company and delicate fare, including, of course, canvasback ducks, done to a turn,—just twenty minutes,—and a small bottle with each bird. The distinguished guest looked at his plate, seemed at a loss, and then leaning across the table said to an American bishop in a tone rather more audible than he used in his lectures: "Bishop, how is it that you *nevah* know how to cook birds in your country?" The bishop blushed, and confessed that he could not quite explain it.

It was what the French call "*une gaffe*," of course: but it was not ill-natured, and therefore not really rude. Who would not pardon a little thing like that to the man who had written *Essays in Criticism*, and *Sohrab and Rustem*, and *Rugby Chapel*, and all the rest of Arnold's fine and noble works?

The truth is, there is a mental and moral kinship between Great Britain and America which makes little differences in manners and occasional infelicities seem of small account. We have the same classics in literature, from the English Bible down. We have been nourished on the same conceptions of self-reliance and fair play, individual liberty and social order. We have the same respect for practical efficiency, though I think the British lay more stress on solidity, the Americans on rapidity, of work. We feel the same aversion from autocracy and disgust for lawlessness. We like to deal with hard facts; but

"We live by admiration, hope, and love."

We resemble each other enough in great things, and differ enough in small, to make a mutual understanding easy, profitable, and durable,—provided we do not suffer the petty politicians to spoil it by frivolous pranks.

Who can doubt that this good understanding has been increasing and deepening through the hundred and seven years of peace between Britain and America? We have had disputes, but they have been settled by the method of reason and justice. A thousand ties of grateful friendship have been woven between British and American homes. The best book on the American Commonwealth has been written by Viscount Bryce, a North Briton;

A CERTAIN INSULARITY

and the best book on the British Constitution by President Lowell of Harvard, a New Englander. Of course there are still things in American humor which the average Britisher does not catch until the next day, and things in British humor which the average Yankee never gets at all. But upon the whole we have learned to "swap jokes" with reciprocal enjoyment. Since the common experience of our soldiers in the great war, fighting side by side in the same cause with France, we have learned that the British are not "a nation of shopkeepers," and they have learned that the Americans are not "a tribe of dollar-worshippers."

Yes, I think they even understand what we mean when we join with them heartily in singing *God Save the King*, but refrain from *Rule Britannia* on the ground that "the tune is unfamiliar."

But there is no reserve nor coolness in our love and admiration for their sea-girt home where our forefathers once lived,—

"A right little, tight little island."

No wonder they are proud of it. From Land's End to John O'Groat's House, from the white cliffs of the Channel to the black crags of Devon and

Wales, from the broads of Lincolnshire to the firths and sounds of Argyle and Ross, from the rolling Downs to the misty Highlands, Earth has nothing better in the way of an island,—

"A precious stone set in the silver sea."

How varied, how rich, how abundant! It is full of shrines and monuments, yet not crammed with them. The sober splendor of the cathedrals, the sense of solid power in the cities, the opulent verdure and bloom of the countryside, the air of permanence and security alike in castle and cottage, the long intimacy and fresh vigor with which Nature responds to the touch of man,—all these things steal upon your heart quietly and irresistibly and make you feel that Great Britain is the most wonderful country in the world next to your own.

Ireland also is an island,—a very beautiful one,—and it has its own insularity. The trouble is that it has two insularities, one to the north, and one to the south. When they are harmonized to desire the same thing it will be a fine day for the Green Isle.

There is a very pretty illustration both of the defects and of the virtues of insularity, in a precious

A CERTAIN INSULARITY

old book. It seems that a certain vessel was wrecked long ago on an island called Malta. The ship was acting, in a way, as a government transport, for she carried a prisoner of state, named Paul, with his military guard. Now their guidepost was marked "Rome." But by reason of the present rain and the cold they had urgent need of a camp-fire. This the islanders kindled, Paul helping them. As he was laying sticks on the flame, a little poison-snake sprang out and fastened on his hand. Whereupon the islanders concluded that he was a murderer pursued by the divine Nemesis. But when he shook off the deadly worm and felt no harm, they promptly changed their minds and said that he was a god. These superstitions and extreme judgments belong to the dangerous side of insularity. But the good side came out when the islanders took the castaways into comfortable winter quarters, entertained them hospitably for three months, and loaded them with useful gifts at their departure.

I have been struck of late by the multitude of unsuspected islands in the world.

Regions supposed to be continental turn out to be surrounded by water. Princeton, New Jersey,

CAMP-FIRES

where I live, is discovered to have an insular quality, being enclosed by two rivers, a canal, and the Atlantic Ocean. The completion of the Panama Canal places the United States on an island. Rather a large one, it is true, but perhaps the subtle influence of this geographical circumstance may have had something to do with a recent acute attack of insularity in the Senate.

In fact, reader, you can make an island out of almost anything, if you wish to. An exclusive creed, an arbitrary taste, a political dogmatism, a closed mind, a dislike for children and dogs, yes, even a passion for musk as a personal perfume, will serve well enough to cut you off from other people if that is what you wish.

But that is certainly the wrong kind of insularity. You might as well be cast away on an uninhabited atoll.

The best islanders, it seems to me, are those who live on their islands not as hermits, nor as pirates, but as good and hospitable neighbors; pleased with their own isle, trying to improve it, and keeping up communications with the rest of the archipelago.

There is a great difference between insularity and isolation.

III

A BASKET OF CHIPS

USE these for your own fire, reader, if you think they are dry enough to make it burn brighter. I don't ask you to agree with me; but let me sit beside you while you prove me wrong. The wet-blanket is the only man I can't endure.

* *

Life is just the process of discovering our relationships. While they increase, we grow. When they diminish, we shrink. There is no death except for those who shut themselves up and out.

* *

First comes a declaration of independence: then a recognition of interdependence.

* *

It is a pity that men should be divided by their pleasures more than by their work.

* *

We have a word for suffering together,—sympathy. But where is the word for rejoicing together?

* *

Every possible form of government has been tried, and found both good and bad. They would

CAMP-FIRES

all be intolerable but for the quiet people who trust in the Lord and do good. They are the only ones who count. Wherefore I believe there is an invisible kingdom which cannot be shaken.

* *

Why quarrel about the social order? It is the social spirit that makes the difference.

* *

I sat next a fat commercial traveller in the smoking-car. He wore large diamonds, knew nothing, and found fault (profanely) with everything except the Russian Soviets and the Sinn Fein Republic. God pity his wife,—unless she was like him.

* *

"Tact," said a witty lady, "is the unsaid part of what you think." Yes, and there is only one thing more potent,—its opposite,—the unthought part of what you say.

* *

In the big woods this is the law: Every trapper must keep to his own line of traps, but the camp-fire is open to all comers. If you are hungry, part of the food belongs to you. But if you take what you don't need, you are a thief and liable to be shot.

* *

Doubt is like fog. It hides things, but it does not destroy them.

* *

It is easier to get what we like than to escape from what we dislike. Good music is not difficult to obtain. But it is hard to get away from the ugly noises with which the modern city is cursed. To open a fine vista you have only to cut a few trees. But to shut out an ugly view you must plant a grove and wait for it to grow. You will teach your children good principles more readily than you will rid them of bad habits.

* *

It is not Bummell's ignorance that offends me. It is his ignoring of his ignorance.

* *

"Cæsar's wife must be above suspicion." Certainly! But how about Cæsar? I know of no proverb more Turkish than this.

* *

'Tis a poor education of which the chief result is the acquisition of prejudices.

* *

CAMP-FIRES

The statesman who always follows public opinion is a pilot who always steers with the tide. He doesn't earn his fee.

* *

The mother of poets is the Earth; their father is the Great Spirit.

IV

SELF, NEIGHBOR, AND COMPANY

IN every one of those ambulant firms doing business in life, which we call human beings, there are three members: the irreducible individual, the social colleague, and the divine silent partner.

The last, it appears, may sometimes be excluded from participation in the affairs of the firm. But in that case there is always a danger that the remaining two, (being by nature as inseparable as the Siamese Twins,) will come to the calamity of a falling-out, in which the interests of one or the other will suffer, or, as more frequently happens, they will decline together toward a common bankruptcy.

This, you will readily perceive, is a metaphorical statement which demands some exercise of the imagination to bring it within the rubric under which the editor of *Scribner's* announced some of these essays,—"comment on *current events*."

The current events that interest me most are not those which glitter upon the surface and attract publicity, nor those which can be "head-lined," nor those which emerged yesterday with a splash and are likely to disappear to-morrow or next day under impermanent ripples; but those which began long ago and promise or threaten to continue a long time, those which are unmarketable as news, those which run beneath the noise and turbulence of clashing waves. In short, I propose to find my themes in *undercurrent events*, and my illustrations as Providence may send them floating along.

Daily happenings can best be understood through a knowledge of human nature. The key to public problems is in the custody of private life.

That is what I want to talk about, and that is why I invite consideration of the fortunes of the old-established, much-imperilled, indispensable firm of Self, Neighbor, and Company.

I

ONE of the chief things we have to do, on arrival in this strange world, is to make our own acquaintance. The baby does not know himself at all when he begins life. He learns to know his food, his ball, his cradle, his mother, other members of the family, even the household cat, before he knows anything about himself.

SELF, NEIGHBOR & CO.

"The baby new to earth and sky,
What time his tender palm is prest
Against the circle of the breast,
Has never thought that 'this is I.'"

When he begins to talk he often shows this limitation in the manner of his speech. He does not say, "I am hungry," "I want so and so." He says "Billy hungry"; "Billy wants"; as if Billy were a simple force of nature. And this, in a certain sense, is all that Billy is at that stage of his growth.

But presently he becomes aware that behind these powers of seeing and hearing, there is some one who sees and hears. Behind these feelings of hunger and cold, there is some one who wants to be fed and warmed. Underneath all these services which his mother and other persons render to the baby, there is a little person whom they love and whom they wish to love them in return. That is a wonderful discovery. The baby becomes his own Christopher Columbus. He finds himself,—his *me*.

Of course it is an unexplored continent,—boundaries, climate, contents, all unknown. But it exists. It is just as real as anything outside of it.

He soon learns to distinguish this little person

from exterior things, even from the house and the body in which he lives. He says "my foot, my hand, my head," claiming ownership, but knowing that neither foot nor hand nor head is himself. He discriminates among the people and other living creatures around him,—some friendly and some hostile. He begins to grasp, rather slowly, the distinction between his own things and the things of others. He learns that the appetites and desires, which at first seemed irresistible powers of nature, are personal to himself and must be controlled in relation to the wants and needs of other persons around him, otherwise disagreeable consequences will ensue. He finds out not only that Billy *is*, but that Billy *belongs*. He exists, but not alone. He is part of a circle of life. Into this circle he must try to fit his new-found self, for joy or sorrow, for good or ill.

It is from this double discovery,—the finding of himself, and the finding of his relation to things and to other persons,—that his whole growth as a man, a thinking, feeling, acting individual, must proceed. His schooling, his pleasures, his friendships, his occupation, his citizenship, everything must be under the wing-and-wing impulse of these two facts: first, that Billy is; and second, that Billy belongs.

SELF, NEIGHBOR & CO.

If we have no real self, no thoughts, no feelings, no personality of our own, we are not persons at all. We are mere parts of a machine.

If on the other hand we are ruled only by self-will, self-interest, we are sure to injure other people, and in the end to destroy our own happiness. We become objectionable members of the community, nuisances, if not criminals.

The most difficult problem in the conduct of life is the harmonizing of these two principles, so that they will work together.

Every one is born an individual, a self; and that self has the right (which is also a duty) to live and grow.

Every one is likewise born a neighbor; with ties and obligations and duties which spread out on all sides. Which has the higher claim? Or are they equal?

In theory it is easy to find an answer sounding well enough. But in practice, when there are only two partners in the firm, they often come to a deadlock and stand bickering in a grievous desperation betwixt the devil of Egoism and the deep sea of Altruism.

Of the two, it must be admitted, the devil has the closer hold on us, but the deep sea is by far the cleaner and less treacherous. Yet I confess to a rooted distrust of all "isms." They imply a surrender of something precious; they hint mutilation and bondage.

Is there no way of breaking the deadlock, of reconciling the apparently conflicting interests and saving the firm? The only way that I can see is through the guidance and authority of the third partner, who is so much wiser and more fair than either of the others, to both of whom, indeed, he is bound by an equal love. To believe this and to act upon it is religion.

Ordinarily, if we speak of religion at all, we use quiet tones and conventional words. But there are times when the want of it haunts us like a passion, burns us like a fever, pierces us to the marrow with unendurable cold. Out of some tragic clash of duty and desire; after some harrowing vision of the widespread sufferings of mankind, some poignant hearing of

> "the fierce confederate storm
> Of sorrow barricadoed evermore
> Within the walls of cities";

under some tense pressure of reproach, regret, and fear; out of our bewilderment and urgent need, we would fain cry aloud, as a confused soul in mortal peril might shout for guidance and help.

But the answer would come then, as it comes now, not in the whirlwind, the earthquake, or the fire, but in a voice of gentle stillness, saying, "Thou shalt love thy neighbor as thyself." Here is balm of Gilead; oil and wine for the broken traveller on the Jericho Road; social wisdom from the fountain-head for the individual and for society. Here is the heavenly plan of the silent partner, to be worked out through all the world's experiments. Without this, none of them can succeed, be it never so angelic. With this, none but the devilish ones can utterly fail.

II

How then are we entitled and bound to love self? That, of course, is the first question, for upon the answer to that depends the line of love which we must follow toward our neighbor.

Said Rabbi Hillel: "If I am not for myself, who will be for me? But if I care for myself only, what am I? And if not now, when?"

Everybody will agree that we must not have a foolish, fond, pampering, spoiling affection for ourselves. We ought not to indulge our own whims and passions, our sloth and selfishness. We ought to dislike and repress that which is evil and mean in us, and to cherish that which is good and generous. The only kind of love for ourselves which is permissible must be wise and clean and careful; it must have justice in it as well as mercy; it must be capable of discipline as well as of encouragement; it must strive to keep the soul above the body, and to develop both.

Precisely thus, and not otherwise, we should love our neighbors: with a steady, sane, liberating and helpful love, which always seeks to bring out their best.

We and they are bound up together in the bundle of life. We cannot advance if they go backward. We cannot be truly happy if they abide in misery. We cannot be really saved if we make no effort to save them. We must withstand in them, just as in ourselves, the things that are evil and ought not to be loved.

Religion does not tell us to love or to encourage our neighbors' faults: but to love *them* in spite of their faults and to do what we can to better them.

True neighbor-love, then, will not be a weak,

SELF, NEIGHBOR & CO.

gelatinous, sentimental thing. It will have a conscience. It will be capable, on occasion, of friendly warning and reproof. It will even accept, if need be for the protection of ourselves and other neighbors, the duty of restraint or punishment. I may have a rowdy or a thief for a neighbor, but my love ought not to embrace rowdiness or thievery in him any more than in myself. The same thing is true of malice or envy or laziness or a slanderous tongue.

But the trouble with us is that our self-reproach is commonly too soft and tender even to pierce the skin, while most of the reproof or restraint or punishment which we give the neighbor is not really animated by love, but by malice, or jealousy, or contempt. That is why it so often fails. It must have good-will back of it and shining through it.

If the people of a community who are thoroughly good in themselves would also be good for others, they would have power to lift up the whole tone of life and would be ten times more happy and more useful.

Doing one's duty on the side of neighborhood leads to the best results on the side of personality.

If a man concentrates his attention and affection and effort on himself, he is not doing the best, but the worst for himself. He is going to be a smooth, self-satisfied prig, or a sour old curmudgeon. Even if he has some kind of a theology it will not do him much good. It is sure to be as narrow and hollow as an empty razor-shell on the beach.

According to the Bible, that kind of theology does not count with God. He cares more for sinners than for the self-righteous. But he cares most for the neighborly folks who try to do right. They are his salt of the earth. They are his lights in the world.

Some Christians are like candles that have been lit once and then put away in a cupboard to be eaten up by mice. How much better to stay lit and keep on burning even till the candle is burned out, so long as it gives light!

There are plenty of us who love ourselves as if we were our own grandmothers. Whenever the little chap cries for more candy, or somebody else's doll, we let him have it. Dear little fellow, he is so cunning!

But the scriptural image of the divine love, which is to be our pattern, is not indulgent grandmotherhood but perfect fatherhood. Now a good father desires each of his children to grow up, to develop.

SELF, NEIGHBOR & CO.

He does not wish them all alike. But he wishes the whole family to have peace and happiness. He wants harmony from the different instruments.

Equality of condition is nowhere written in the Christian programme. In fact the parable of the talents implies a continuing state of inequality.

Yet the real curse of the one-talent man is not the poverty of his portion, but the meanness and selfishness of his heart. He is a slacker, a shirker, a striker, a lock-out man, a parasite. His unused talent becomes a fungus.

That the rich and the poor are likely to be with us as long as men differ in ability and industry, is clearly intimated in the Good Book as well as in the dry tables of political economy. But the Good Book adds a prediction of woe to the rich if they suffer the pride of wealth to divide them from the poor.

"Go to, now, ye rich men, weep and howl for your miseries that shall come upon you. Your riches are corrupted and your garments are motheaten. Your gold and silver is cankered; and the rust of them shall be a witness against you, and shall eat your flesh as it were fire."

Let the economist write this into his tables; it is

essential to the correctness of his computations for this world as well as for the next.

Outward equality of goods without the spirit of neighborliness is equivalent to an inward community of evils. I cannot imagine a state more like hell, this side of Russia. Yet even in Russia the outward equality is a sham, a gross and palpable fraud. Who will assert so much as a decent semblance of parity between Lenine fattening in his stolen palace and Andreyef starving to death in exile?

Charity is scorned and derided by the modern communist. He will none of it. But who can conceive a social order, framed of the present human stuff, in which kindness will not be desirable, necessary, and beautiful?

Kindness is more than mercy tempering justice. It is love thoughtless of reward. It is that godlike impulse which gives to others not barely what they have earned, but what they need.

None of us can get through life without needing charity and longing for it; and there is much comfort in the promise that if we show it on earth we shall find it in Heaven.

SELF, NEIGHBOR & CO.

III

War, with its attendant horrors, seems like an outrage upon love. And so it is, in its origin and source. "From whence come wars and fightings among you? Come they not hence, even of your lusts that war in your members? Ye lust and have not: ye kill, and desire to have, and cannot obtain."

Yet there is a war against war which is set in the very key of "Love thy neighbor as thyself." It was to frustrate a gigantic crime and to redress villainous wrong that the Allies took up arms in the World War, and America at last joined them. Had her heart been quicker, her feet more swift, she might have reached the Jericho Road in time to stop the robbers before they began their cruel work. Who can tell? At least, having arrived, she did her best and beat them off.

Great sacrifice, but far greater reward, came to America in the doing of that clear duty. Never were "we, the people of the United States," so thoroughly united as in that vast co-operation. Not only in mobilizing all our forces and resources for the urgent business of battle, but also in utilizing all the powers of sympathy and help that rust unused in men, women, and children, for the Good Samaritan work of Red Cross and Relief Commission, we learned what it means to be born a neighbor as well as a person.

The self-sufficiency, not to say self-complacency, of the American temperament was absorbed and fused into something larger and better. For a while we ceased to satisfy ourselves with "paddle your own canoe," and took up the finer motto, "for the good of the ship."

With all its trials, privations, and sorrows,—yes, even despite its individual exposures of greed and graft,—the war-time was a time of elevation and enlargement of spirit for the people of America.

Why not carry these benefits of a just war well won, with us into the time of peace? Why not keep the lesson learned at such a cost? No man, no community, no nation liveth to self alone.

Joubert has well said: "To wish to do without other men and to be under obligation to no one, is a sure mark of a mind devoid of feeling." To this I would add: A mind devoid of feeling never reasons right in the affairs of life, because feeling is a vital element of sound reasoning.

SELF, NEIGHBOR & CO.

IV

Two philosophies have long contended for the control of thought. One is called Individualism, because it lays the emphasis upon the single person, his rights, privileges, liberties, happiness. The other is called Socialism, because it lays the emphasis on the community. The partisans of these two theories fight each other furiously.

It seems to me that both theories are wrong, when they are interpreted exclusively and with damnatory clauses. Each has a ray of truth in it when it takes account of the other.

The most perfect type of individualism is the "rogue" elephant,—solitary, predatory, miserable,—a torment to himself and a terror to others.

The most perfect example of pure socialism is a swarm of bees, where personality is *nil*, every member gets the same pay,—board and lodging,—and the only object is to perpetuate the swarm and keep the hive full.

But without the aid of man they never produce a better bee or a more perfect hive. Is humanity to come down to that level?

The Talmud speaks scorn of a world where "one

man eats and another says grace." Is it much better than a world where everybody gorges and nobody says grace?

I can see no reason, either in morals or in religion, for the perpetuation of the human swarm, except for the development and perfecting of the human souls who make mankind. What real good appears in the mere continuance of any community, say New York or Nyack, unless you think of the men and women and children who live there, each one the inheritor of a spark of the Divine Life, which may be cherished and enlarged into a flame of beautiful and potent light? There is your reason for sacrifice. There is your reason for service. The community has a claim to live for the sake of the better men and women who are going to live in it and make it better.

So then, amid the confusion at the present cross-roads where the counsels of the many are so loud and divergent, we find a little neglected guide-post. Look, 'tis so old and weather-beaten that some of the letters are worn away; yet the sense of it is still legible:

LOVE—NEIGHBOR—SELF

SELF, NEIGHBOR & CO.

It reads like a general order.

Suppose we should try one of these roads marked "Government Ownership" or "Collective Bargaining" or "High Productiveness" or "Independence of Employers" or "Control by Employees," and find that it was leading us away from our objective. Might not the order nerve us to turn back?

Or, if the road seemed to be a right one, evidently bringing us nearer to our objective, wouldn't the order encourage us to carry on, and cheer us through the hardships of the way?

Let no one imagine that it will be easy. A general order is far more difficult to follow than a definite programme. Most men prefer a concrete dose of medicine, however bitter, to a long course of hygienic living.

To live up to a principle is harder than to obey a rule. But just for that reason it may be better.

Let us try it, Self and Neighbor, try it more seriously than we have yet done. The drop of good-will in all our experiments! The touch of kindness in all our efforts! The purpose of beneficence in all our plans! For a year, a month, even a week,—do you think we can do it?

You are my partner, and I am yours. But to tell

CAMP-FIRES

the truth, between us we have small capital and less experience. To carry out this enterprise we shall need the help of our third partner,—the divine silent one who knows all.

V

SYMPATHETIC ANTIPATHIES

BEING by conviction as well as by profession an adherent of the creed of good-will and an advocate of universal charity, I am not a little chagrined to discover, (and hereby confess,) the considerable part which distastes and antipathies play in my life.

My likings are strong enough to give assurance of health. The charms of a wooded mountain country and swift-flowing streams; American elm-trees, white pines, and silver birches; the taste of fresh asparagus, green peppers, and bacon; the company of frank, lively, sensible, and unenvious people; the reading of books well written on subjects worth writing about;—to all these and many other attractions I am open and pliable, without much reasoning or moral suasion.

On the other hand my dislikings, though less numerous, are quite as strong. A flat, bald country, dry or damp; dumplings, veal, and salt codfish; a clay soil; a lymphatic temperament in a woman, and a sour, jealous disposition in a man; books about nothing, written in a sloppy or pretentious style—these are things that I cannot abide.

Nor am I greatly concerned to justify such-like repugnancies by abstract reasoning or high ethical or political considerations. They belong to the sphere of personal privilege. Without some admixture of this kind, temperamental rather than logical, we can hardly maintain our existence as real individuals. Mankind, thus denatured, would be reduced to the dreary stratifications of class-consciousness. Given the label of his church, or political party, or handicraft, or profession, you could predict precisely what your quasi-man would be and do. The more eminent in his type, the more sapless and savorless would he be in his person. He would resemble that modern statue which Julius Hare describes in "Guesses at Truth": "Like the yolk of an egg cased in the soft albumen of a pseudo-ideal."

A man refined or sublimated beyond a capacity for simple, natural dislikes is distinctly not a likable character. Beneath the glossy surface of a superior neutrality in minor things, he may hide a major hatred, a fixed, unalterable enmity, irrational as the jaundice and implacable as a vendetta.

Give me rather the man of frank though foolish

SYMPATHETIC ANTIPATHIES

aversions; the man who protests that he knows nothing about art but is quite sure of what he does *not* like, and declines to be bothered with it; the man who has no better cause to give for his repugnancy to So-and-So than that his mouth is cut the wrong way, or that he talks through his nose and pronounces "programme" to rhyme with "pogrom." These are pardonable prejudices. They are to be placed in the necessary, non-moral region of human life. They belong to the domain of unaccountable reactions, covered by the classic quatrain,—

> "I do not love thee, Doctor Fell,
> The reason why I cannot tell;
> But this alone I know full well,
> I do not love thee, Doctor Fell."

Now, the subject of these famous lines was an eminently respectable scholar and prelate, dean of Christ Church, and afterward Bishop of Oxford, in the seventeenth century. The author of the lines was one Tom Brown, a student at Christ Church, and a vagarious fellow whom Addison characterized as "of Facetious Memory." Yet I am prepared to defend the irregular Tom Brown in his confession that he disliked the established John Fell without as-

CAMP-FIRES

signable reasons. At all events, but for this whimsical antipathy the name of Doctor Fell would never have become a household word. So far, it benefited him. But what it did to handicap Tom Brown's academic career, we know not.

It must be admitted, for candor's sake, that these unreasoned dislikes are not generally profitable in the affairs of life. They act as restraints and inhibitions: whether wise or not, God alone knoweth that alloweth them.

I recall that my father, (of blessed memory,) had an aversion from an unknown man whom he used to meet and pass in his morning walks in the city of Brooklyn, going at a certain hour through Remsen Street from his house to his study in the church which he served. This man he pointed out to me once as we walked together. He was quite an ordinary citizen, tailor-made, glum-faced, sour-looking, with a white patch over one eye, and of a general scorbutic appearance, unpleasant but not terrifying. Yet my father felt so strong a detestation for the mere look of the man, that he regarded it as ominous and malign, and fell into the habit of walking around by way of Montague Street, rather than risk meeting his *bête noire* in Remsen Street.

SYMPATHETIC ANTIPATHIES

It was absurd no doubt, but not reprehensible; and it had one good result,—a little longer exercise for my father in the fresh air every morning.

My own dislikings have often demanded payment for their indulgence. What shall a man who abhors veal, and believes that if he eats it he will presently faint away and perhaps die of acute indigestion,—what shall such a man do at the *tables-d'hôte* of Europe? He must practise vegetarianism, or bribe the waiter to procure a substitute for the unleavened *Kalbfleisch*.

My absolute inability to love flat and treeless countries, my positive aversion from sage-brush and alkali, have prevented me from sharing the eloquent affection of my Cousin John for *The Desert*. He may have it all if he likes. Also he may have the paintings of Matisse, and the plays of the very Belgian Shakespeare, Maeterlinck, and the anthologies of Spoon River and other level and bald localities, if they please him. To me they are as veal, and clay, and salt codfish. *Je m'en fiche.* Poorer this abstinence may make me, but it leaves me honest. And it does not deprive me of the pleasure of admiring the gusto, (to use Hazlitt's word,) with which my Cousin John praises the desert and finds excuse for its lack of eyebrows and eyelashes in the wondrous lights reflected in its ever-open eyes. By proxy I enjoy it through his enjoyment.

> "But not for all his faith can see,
> Would I that desert-dweller be."

Here we approach, by a devious but necessary detour, the particular subject of this paper. Dislikes, aversions, repugnancies, are inevitable, and therefore to a certain extent defensible. But only those are wholesome and profitable which have in them a little ray of comprehension, a little drop of love.

Trust not your antipathies unless they are sympathetic.

Do you remember how Charles Lamb begins his essay on "All Fools' Day"?

"The compliments of the season to my worthy masters, and a merry first of April to *us all!*"

How often, if we have the priceless art of being sincere with ourselves, do we recognize in the qualities which displease us in others, the very imps and unruly sprites which cause the most trouble in our own interior economy! At home we are inclined

SYMPATHETIC ANTIPATHIES

to go gently with them, to make allowances, even to plead excuse for our bothersome offspring. And who shall say that this is altogether wrong or absolutely unwise? Many a vice is but a virtue overdriven. Pruning is better than extermination.

But why not apply the same principle to what we see in our neighbor's back garden, or in his front yard? Why not remember that he probably has as much trouble with his faults and foibles as we have with our own? And if they happen to be alike, why not use them for self-enlightenment and correction?

The things that we dislike in others may serve as mirrors to ourselves. But let us not follow the example of that foolish person described in the Epistle of St. James, who "beholding his natural face in a glass, goeth his way and straightway forgetteth what manner of man he was."

Take that tendency to quick and fierce anger which the Romans called *iracundia*, and in later Latin *stomachatio*, as if it were a sudden rising of the gorge. We call it irascibility. It is not a lovable quality. Yet those of us who are afflicted with it would not really admit that it is only and altogether evil. We would plead the excuses of righteous wrath; we would claim that good fuel answers quickly to the flame; we would say, as if it were a complete justification, "you knew I had a hasty temper; why did you provoke me?"

Suppose we should apply to others the same arguments and palliations that we use for ourselves. Suppose that the great quarrel of to-day between two irascible men, in which the interests of all nations and of many millions of mankind are involved, should have its natural antipathies loosened and resolved by the infusion of a good-humored drop of sympathy. Would it not have a happy effect?

I like the advice of Plutarch in the third volume of his "Morals," where he says, "Should you quarrel with your brother, *avoid intercourse with his enemies, and hold correspondence with his friends.*"

This seems to be a practical comment on the words of St. Paul, wherein we find both a reasonable concession to the infirmity of our human tempers and a Christian counsel for controlling them. "Be ye angry," says he, quite positively, as if we could not help it, "and sin not. Let not the sun go down upon your wrath."

Anger that breaks out is troublesome. Anger that sinks in is fatal.

SYMPATHETIC ANTIPATHIES

A well-founded mistrust of treacherous persons we may keep. But God save us from the poison of a cherished grudge.

Consider in like manner, the foible of vanity. Nothing is more apt to evoke antipathy, *especially in those who are tinctured with the same fault*.

The arrival of a person with a too manifest good opinion of himself in a small community where conceit is endemic, seems like a direct challenge to all the legitimate inheritors of self-complacency. It becomes their pleasure as well as their duty to meet the emergency and to rescue their neighbor from his annoying sin.

Sometimes they go about it with open ridicule, which is wholesome and harmless enough, if it be free from malice. At other times a kind of League to Enforce Humility is silently formed and everybody is proud to have a modest part in its work.

The best leader in such a campaign of levelling improvement is usually a female who has passed middle age in unquestioned respectability and has established a local reputation for mordant wit. Being cased in the defensive armor of self-satisfaction, she is the more free to let fly at random with her sharp-pointed tongue.

CAMP-FIRES

An aged dame of this type I once knew, who was a terror to the fresh and exuberant, and a perpetual joy to herself. She was a past mistress in the art of making people feel uncomfortable when she thought they needed it. For those who crossed her path in the flush of a first success or in the glow of some long task finally accomplished, she had the vigilant eye of a sleepless monitor, and the swift, unerring weapon of a winged and barbed word. After such a discharge you could see her fluffing her feathers and preening herself like a hen who has just performed the miracle of laying an egg. "Aha," she seemed to say, "did you watch me do that? How neatly I brought that cockscomb down! Vanity is a thing that I cannot endure."

One is reminded of the great word which George Meredith, in "The Egoist," makes Sir Willoughby Patterne utter to Clara, his hapless fiancée: "Beware of marrying an Egoist, my dear!"

An English rhymer has a verse on this subject:

> The hunters of Conceit pursue a fox
> Endowed with magic that deludes and mocks;
> He doubles, turns, and ere they end the race,
> Each dog that follows wears a foxy face;
> The scent they ran by on themselves is found,
> And now they chase each other round and round.

SYMPATHETIC ANTIPATHIES

The wisest and most amiable of mankind are always aware of this subtle and tricksy quality of conceit, which masquerades in our Sunday clothes and peeps out at us from our own photographs. Doth not Michel de Montaigne, after humbly acknowledging that he has no memory, mollify that self-accusation by remarking that "it is commonly seene by experience that excellent memories do rather accompany weake judgements"? Bravo, intrepid philosopher of Perigord and writer of the most frankly ingenuous essays ever penned! Why should we take umbrage at your further confession? "Glorie and curiositie are the scourges of our soules. The one induceth us to have an oare in every ship, and the other forbiddeth us to leave anything unresolved or undecided."

Listen also to a more reverend doctor, Blaise Pascal, of Paris and Port Royal. "We toil without ceasing," says he, "to adorn and to uphold our imaginary self, while we neglect our true self altogether. We would gladly act as poltroons to acquire the reputation of being brave. Those who write against glory would fain have the glory of having written well. Those who read them would fain have the glory of having read. *And I, who am writing this, perhaps I also have the same desire. And you, who read, perhaps you will have it also.* Curiosity is nothing but vanity. Generally one wishes to know merely in order to talk about it."

This is an admirable, thoroughgoing discourse, wherein the preacher includes himself with the congregation, and admits, smiling, that humor is not out of place in a serious sermon.

Come from behind your pillar, brother Humilio! Seek not to evade your spoonful of the medicine. Come out, and let us all laugh together and repent and try to mend our ways.

'Tis no new discovery, this streak of vainglory running all through the stuff of our humanity. Plutarch lets in the light upon it when he notes that those who praise an obscure life seek to win fame by their praise of it. He compares them to watermen "who look astern while they row the boat ahead, still so managing the strokes of the oar that the vessel may make on to its port." A few paragraphs later, he goes even beyond this and praises outright the men who seek honor and good repute. "Would you have them out of the way," he asks ironically, "for fear they should set others a good example, and allure others to virtue out of emulation of the precedent?"

SYMPATHETIC ANTIPATHIES

Undoubtedly there is a popular antipathy to those who evidently aim at eminence. Paul Elmer More, in one of his delightful Shelburne essays, describes it as a lurking malady of the democratic spirit, "a kind of *malaise* at distinction, wherever seen and however manifested."

Against this I think we should be on our guard and protect ourselves by whatever prophylactic we can find, just as carefully as against the far more open fault of vanity. Indeed this uneasy resentment at excellence is a covert form of vanity,— *vanitas vulgi*, which cries with the Irishman "One man is as good as another, and better too! Down wid all top-hats!"

It is to this ingrowing self-flattery of democracies rather than to the so-called ingratitude of republics that I would ascribe much of the niggling detraction that has followed many great men in our country. First, a brilliant burst of applause; then a steady rain of abuse; then, (after the man is dead,) a clearing sky and a worthy monument.

Washington, who liberated the country, was accused of truckling to the British and tyrannizing over the Americans. Lincoln, who preserved the Union, was accused of currying favor with the South because he declined to "hang Jeff Davis to a sour apple-tree," or perform other vengeful antics at the bidding of the Yankee irreconcilables. Roosevelt, who preached and practised Americanism on a four-square basis, was called a "grand-stand player," because he evidently relished the plaudits which followed a brave speech or a good stroke. And now Woodrow Wilson is accused of the same heinous crime of grand-stand play because he has plainly sought the honor of promoting the largest plan to defend peace on earth that the world has ever seen. Would that some of those who gibe and fleer at him might betray in themselves a like ambition, an equal willingness to toil, to put aside ease and comfort, to imperil health and life itself for the sake of realizing an ideal whose nobility and generous daring none can deny.

Grand-stand players, forsooth! Then so was Nelson a grand-stand player when he cried at Cape St. Vincent "Westminster Abbey or Victory." So was William of Orange when he aimed to win, and won, from all his people the more than kingly title of "Father." So was Themistocles, the savior of Athens, when he plainly took delight in the applause of the stadium, and showed himself *philotimotatos*, a lover of honor. So has every true hero and notable

SYMPATHETIC ANTIPATHIES

benefactor been of the company of those who labor to deserve, and are not ashamed to enjoy, the approval of their fellow men, if it come on the path of duty and in obedience to the divine command. By such renown their power for good is increased, and the radiance of their example is shed abroad like the light of a candle set on a high place.

Therefore I would not be among the detractors of the great or the minifiers of the illustrious. But the same trouble and toil which those criticasters give themselves to bedim good names and find or paint blots on fair 'scutcheons, would I gladly take to brighten the shield of virtue, to find the most favorable interpretation of the errors of the wise, and to discover new reasons for the admiration of the excellent. Well spoke Jesus the son of Sirach when he said: "Let us now praise famous men, and our fathers that begat us; leaders of the people by their counsels, and by their understanding men of learning for the people; all these were honored in their generations, and were a glory in their days."

But from these heights let us return to the case of Themistocles. It offers an amusing illustration of the vagaries of vanity in human nature. It appears that when the battle of Salamis had been gloriously won under his leadership, a council was held to award the supreme prize of valor. Every general present voted for himself as FIRST in valor; but all voted for Themistocles as SECOND. So the prize was given to him. And I imagine that it was done with general laughter and good humor.

In fact, the only kind of vanity in ourselves that is dangerous is that which cannot endure to be laughed at. And the only kind of vanity in others that is intolerable is that which denies itself to friendly callers, assumes an *alias*, and puts on the ragged cloak and broken sandals of a mock humility. All other kinds are tolerable; and if we are honest and mindful of our own infirmity, we can but feel toward them a sympathetic antipathy.

There are many other common faults and failings besides vanity, which we dislike in our neighbors and for which we may find some explanation, if not excuse, if we will but look more closely into ourselves.

Does Grandioso exaggerate? Truly, it is a grievous habit. But have not you, dear Piscator, an inclination to round out your fish-stories with an extra pound? You do it for the pleasure of your

SYMPATHETIC ANTIPATHIES

hearers, of course, but will you not allow the same palliation to your friend?

Dogmatism is antipathetic to most men. Yet there is hardly one of us who will not "lay down the law" when he gets on his favorite subject. So much the better, if we avoid sentences and penalties for unbelief.

To tell you of all the things to which my antipathies are sympathetic would be too long a tale. It would amount to a last confession and a judgment-day account. It would not interest you. The camp-fire of this night burns low. Before it goes out, let us turn back to our most common failing and universal antipathy, vanity, and see if we can find a little guide-post on the way out.

For the mitigation and restraint of conceit, when it becomes acute (either in its gratified or its ungratified form), there is no better remedy than to frequent the company of little people to whom your occupation and your achievements (or failures) are unknown. Elsewhere you may find heating flattery, or freezing contempt. But here you may forget your wounds and cool your fever in that fresh and impartial air which belongs to the society of young children. If the little ones see you sad, they will

CAMP-FIRES

give you a glance of sorrow, they know not why, and then demand a new story. If they see you glad, they will rejoice with you, they know not why, and then call you to their merriest play. It is helpful to get away from yourself.

Let the writer forsake his Poetry Societies and Authors' Leagues, and go into the woods where the lumbermen and guides and hunters have never heard of his books, and yet manage to live with some joy. Let the captain of industry or finance take a little voyage among the fishermen who know nothing of his triumphs or defeats on the Exchange. Let the professor find friends among farmers or commercial travellers who ignore the difference between Q.E.D. and Ph.D. Let the artist forsake the academy or Greenwich Village for some region where his shibboleth is never spoken because it cannot be pronounced.

And the politician,—where shall he go, in this age of democracy? Merciful heaven, I know not,—unless it be to a Trappist monastery,—or, better still, among the little children, who are too young to have votes and too wise to seek offices.

VI

PUBLICOMANIA

It is a strange thing to see how deeply certain people of our time have been smitten with a form of insanity which we may call, for want of a dictionary word, publicomania. The name is rather ugly, and altogether irregular, being of mixed Latin and Greek descent. But it is no worse than the thing it describes, which is, in fact, a sort of mongrel madness. It has some kinship with the Roman Grandio's passion for celebrity which Seneca satirized, and not a little likeness to the petty ostentation of Beau Tibbs at which Goldsmith laughed kindly in London a century ago.

But in our own day the disease has developed a new symptom. It is not enough to be pointed out with the forefinger of notoriety: the finger which points must be stained with printer's ink. The craving for publicity is not satisfied with anything but a paragraph in the newspapers; then it wants a column; and finally it demands a whole page with illustrations. The delusion consists in the idea that a sufficient quantity of this kind of notoriety amounts to fame.

It is astonishing to observe how much time, ingenuity, money, and vital energy, people who are otherwise quite sane, will spend for the sake of having their names and unimportant doings chronicled, in a form of print which can be preserved only in private and very inconvenient scrap-books. In England, where they have a hereditary aristocracy and a *Court Journal*, the mania seems less difficult to understand. But in this country, where the limits of the "smart set" are confessedly undefined and indefinable, changing with the fluctuations of the stock-market and the rise and fall of real estate, it is impossible to conceive what benefit or satisfaction reasonable beings can derive from a temporary enrolment among the assistants at fashionable weddings, the guests at luxurious banquets, or the mourners at magnificent funerals.

Our wonder increases when we consider that there is hardly a detail of private life, from the cradle to the grave, which is not now regarded as appropriate for publication, provided only the newspapers are induced to take an interest in it. The interest of the public is taken for granted. Formerly the

PUBLICOMANIA

intrusion of reporters into such affairs was resented. Now it is their occasional neglect to intrude which causes chagrin.

If we could suppose that all this was only a subtle and highly refined mode of advertisement, it would be comparatively easy to account for it. There would be method in the madness. But why in the world should a man or a woman care to advertise things which are not to be sold—a wedding trousseau, the decorations of a bedroom, a dinner to friends, or the flowers which conceal a coffin? We can see well enough why a dealer in old silver should be pleased at having his wares described in the newspapers. But what interest has Mr. Newman Biggs in having the public made aware of the splendor and solidity of his plate?

Of course one must recognize that there is such a thing as public life. It is natural and reasonable that those who are engaged in it should accept publicity, and even seek it within proper limits, so far as it may be a necessary condition of success in their work. Authors and artists wish to have their books read and their pictures looked at. Statesmen and reformers desire to have their policies and principles discussed. Benefactors of mankind wish at least to have their schools and hospitals and libraries received with as much attention as may be needed to make them useful.

But why the people who are chiefly occupied in eating and drinking, marrying and giving in marriage, should wish to have their lives turned inside out on the news-stands passes comprehension. They subject themselves to all the inconveniences of royalty (being, as Montaigne says, "in all the daily actions of life encircled and hemmed in by an importunate and tedious multitude"), without any of its compensations. They are exposed by their own fantastic choice to what Cowley called "a quotidian ague of frigid impertinences," and they get nothing for it but the disadvantage of being talked about. The result of their labors and sufferings is simply to bring them to the condition of a certain Doctor William Kenrick, of whom old Samuel Johnson said, "Sir, he is one of those who have made themselves public without making themselves known."

But if we are inclined to be scornful of the vagaries of publicomania, this feeling must surely be softened into something milder and more humane when we reflect upon the unhappy state of mind to which it reduces those who are afflicted with it. They are

PUBLICOMANIA

not as other men, to whom life is sweet for its own sake. The feasts to which they are bidden leave them hungry unless their presence is recorded in the *Daily Eavesdropper*. They are restless in their summer rest unless their comings and goings are printed in the chronicle of fashionable intelligence. Their new houses do not please them if the newspaper fails to give sufficient space to the announcement that they are "at home." It is a miserable condition, and one from which all obscure and happy persons should pray to be delivered.

There is, however, consolation for true lovers of humanity in the thought that the number of people who are afflicted with this insanity in an incurable form is comparatively small. They make a great noise, like Edmund Burke's company of vociferous grasshoppers under a leaf in the field where a hundred cattle are quietly feeding; but, after all, the great silent classes are in the majority. The common sense of mankind agrees with the poet Horace in his praise of the joys of retirement:

"*Secretum iter, et fallentis semita vitæ.*"

One of the best antidotes and cures of the craze for publicity is a love of poetry and of the things that belong to poetry—the beauty of nature, the sweetness and splendor of the common human affections, and those high thoughts and unselfish aspirations which are the enduring treasures of the soul.

It is good to remember that the finest and most beautiful things that can ever come to us cannot possibly be news to the public. It is good to find the zest of life in that part of it which does not need, and will not bear, to be advertised. It is good to talk with our friends, knowing that they will not report us; and to play with the children, knowing that no one is looking at us; and to eat our meat with gladness and singleness of heart. It is good to recognize that the object of all true civilization is that a man's house, rich or poor, shall be his castle, and not his dime museum. It is good to enter into the spirit of Wordsworth's noble sonnet, and, turning back to "the good old cause," thank God for those safeguards of the private life which still preserve in many homes

"Our peace, our fearful innocence,
And pure religion breathing household laws."

VII

MOVING DAY

LONG ago in Brooklyn,—in the consulship of Plancus, when Fernando Wood was Tammany Mayor of New York, and the irrepressible effervescence of the Fenians bubbled over in antidraft riots,—in that rolled-golden age, May Day was "Moving Day."

Beautiful Brooklyn, with breezy Heights overlooking the turbulent tides of East River, and the round green patch of Governor's Island, and the long low metropolis of Manhattan, and the hills of New Jersey and Staten Island beyond the busy harbor! What a broad and noble outlook, what a rural self-complacent charm was thine, O city of churches, "all unravaged by the fierce intellectual life of the century," wrapped in New England traditions and based on a solid Dutch financial foundation!

Beecher and Storrs were thine, Jachin and Boaz, pillars of the oratorical Temple,—and, Lord, how they hated each other! Walt Whitman also was thine, the insurgent rhapsodical poet,—but thou knewest him not because he was flannel-shirted. Placid and prim were thy streets, and thy spirit was self-contented, sure that the ultimate truth and the final social form were embodied in Brooklyn.

(Reader, I am afraid that these paragraphs, if you follow the punctuation, may seem like uncapitalized *vers libre*. Let us get back to honest prose.)

May the first, in the days which I recall, was the time appointed for the migration of households.

It was not a movable feast, it was a fixed feast of movables.

The little houses poured forth their accumulated treasures and rubbish to be conveyed to other little houses. "Apartments" were unknown, but tenements had begun to exist. Neither the origin nor the destination made any difference. The point was that you had to move if your lease was up; and your goods and chattels had to move with you.

Great was the disclosure, on that day, of the stuff that had been accumulated. The discreet, gigantic moving-van had not yet been invented. Everything must be carried in more or less open carts and wagons. The ramshackle, the unnecessary, the futile, in the household gear, was inevitably

MOVING DAY

betrayed. Moving Day was more or less a day of confession and repentance.

Even solid and useful articles of furniture,—sofas of age if not of antiquity, armchairs and rockers, centre-tables and dinner-tables, double bedsteads and writing-desks,—have a forlorn, disreputable air when they are turned upside down. Their legs project helplessly. They look inebriate. Their accustomed use, the dignity of their position, the softening and concealing aid of lambrequins and portières, antimacassars and footstools, fringed lamp-shades and mantel ornaments,—all the paraphernalia of their domestic state are stripped away from them. In the language of the prophets, "their nakedness is uncovered." The broken leg, the cracked foot-board, the scratched surface, the worn covering, the huge rent and the broken spring underneath the corner of the parlor sofa,—all are bared to the cold light of day and the unsympathetic comment of the casual passer-by.

Worst of all is the state of the enormous, unwieldy, beloved, square piano. For this, usually, a separate dray and special movers are necessary,—men of rugged aspect and profane speech, men who "have no music in their souls," who care not for the sweet harmonies evoked from that gigantic rosewood box when Amelia played "The Wakening of the Lion," or "The Maiden's Prayer," or "Juanita," and eager swains stood near her to turn the leaves. The melodious monster now lies prone like a stricken hippopotamus: its huge carved and convoluted legs are dismembered. Beside it in the dray reposes its faithful little satellite, the piano-stool, with feet uplifted as if in mute appeal.

Among the *disjecta membra* were many things that in later times will rarely be seen, unless a place is found for them in the museums of antiquity where spinning-wheels and warming-pans are assembled. There were the long tin bathtubs, painted green without and white within, and their little round brothers, the foot-tubs of like complexion. There were enclosed wash-stands, with cupboards beneath, where articles of domestic virtue could be concealed, and with rods above, on which embroidered "splashers" portraying one-legged storks could be displayed. There were portentous parlor-lamps on lofty brass pedestals, and curious candelabra adorned with prismatic glass pendants. All these, and other things of like nature, modern plumbing and gas-fitting and electric wiring have consigned

MOVING DAY

to the species of creatures extinct or soon to be extinguished. But for the time being they had their place with the fearfully and wonderfully made "chromos," and the Rogers clay-statuettes, and the red-plush family albums,—among the impedimenta which the mid-Victorian household chose to encumber itself on the pilgrimage of life.

Moving Day brought them all out. To us children, when it struck our own family, it was a time of excitement, and of apprehension lest our own particular treasurable rubbish should be forgotten or broken. But when it struck other families, we found it a time of curiosity and amusement. We never thought of questioning its reason or its necessity. To us it seemed like something between a joke and a law of nature.

Since then I have tried to discover, in a mildly historical spirit, the connection between this feast of movables and the first day of May,—a point of time more naturally associated with outdoor sports and pastimes in the joyousness of returning spring.

The dull, obvious, logical answer to these inquiries would be that since leases were made and expired "as of May first," that was inevitably the day to move if the lease was not renewed. But the deeper question still remains: *why did the leases fix that day?*

Washington Irving, in his "Knickerbocker History of New York," professes to give an exact historical explanation. It was on the first of May, says he, that the original Dutch settlers of the New Netherlands removed from their first establishment on the marshy lands of Communipaw, west of the Hudson, to the more salubrious and pleasant island of Mannahatta.

"Houses were turned inside out, and stripped of all the venerable furniture which had come from Holland. . . . By degrees a fleet of boats and canoes were piled up with all kinds of household articles; ponderous tables; chests of drawers resplendent with brass ornaments; quaint corner cupboards; beds and bedsteads; with any quantity of pots, kettles, frying-pans and Dutch ovens. In each boat embarked a whole family, from the robustious burgher down to the cats and dogs and little negroes. . . . This memorable migration took place on the first of May, and was long cited in tradition as the *grand moving*. The anniversary of it was piously observed among the 'sons of the Pilgrims of Communipaw,' by turning their houses

MOVING DAY

topsyturvy and carrying all the furniture through the streets, in emblem of the swarming of the parent hive; and this is the real origin of the universal agitation and 'moving' by which this most restless of cities is literally turned out of doors on every May-day."

Graphic and humorous explanation! But Professor Schele de Vere, of the University of Virginia, who quoted it in his very entertaining book "Americanisms" (1871), was not entirely satisfied with it. "The custom," says he, "is older than the ancient settlement called Communipaw. The Dutch settlers evidently brought it with them from their transatlantic home, and to this day, in Bruges and its neighborhood, in Verviers and many other parts of Belgium and Holland, the first of May continues to be the general day of moving."

No doubt the professor was right. I have seen something of the kind quite recently in the Dutch cities. And no doubt when this essay has been printed and read in various regions, letters will come, (to my delight,) from friendly correspondents, pointing out that the custom of Moving Day was not confined to the districts around New York, and that it is altogether too narrow to ascribe it to a purely Netherlandish origin. Right you are, friend. Granted beforehand! The origin lies in the universal heart of humanity, and in the laws of nature.

Man is a mover. Spring is the time when he feels it.

Since Abraham went down at the divine call from Haran to Canaan, (but Terah stayed in Haran because he liked it better;) since the pious Æneas took old father Anchises out of burning Troy on his back and set sail for Italy; since the Longbeards came into Lombardy, and the Huns into Hungary, and the Romans, Danes, Normans, and others into Great Britain to make up the far-famed "Anglo-Saxon" race; since the Pilgrims, Puritans, Cavaliers, Huguenots, Dutchmen and other folks crossed the ocean with their household gear to occupy new habitations in America; since a time when the memory of man runneth not to the contrary, there has been a terrible amount of moving in the world. It seems like a nervous habit. And I will wager that when it was not otherwise constrained by circumstances it has usually shown itself most strongly in the vernal season,—that is, in the north temperate zone, somewhere about May first.

MOVING DAY

Understand, I am not now referring to nomads and their vagrant tribes. They are people whose only idea of permanence is a ceaseless wandering. But the folks of whom I speak are house-builders and home-lovers. They want a roof, and a hearthstone or some kind of a substitute. But they are unwilling to be bound to it, or perhaps they are unable to hold on to it, indefinitely.

Sometimes they are forced out, with bitter sorrow, by the relentless hand of avarice, or by the bloody fist of war. There is no sight more pitiful than an evicted family, unless it be a family in flight before a cruel and lustful conqueror,—such as I have seen by thousands upon the roads of France and Belgium in the late world-war.

But more often these migrations, in peaceful times, are the result of altered conditions in industry and trade; or of a desire for an improved situation, or a finer climate, or a more convenient dwelling; or perhaps merely of a subconscious wish for a change, in the hope that it will mean a betterment.

Partially civilized man, if we consider him in the light of self-knowledge, is evidently a home-making creature with migratory instincts.

I admit that there are exceptions, or, to be more

exact, cases in which the home-keeping affection outweighs and overmasters the wandering impulse. That is my own case, though I have come to it late in life. I like my old camp of Avalon, with its big trees, and the marble bird-bath in the garden, and the tall pillars of the verandahs. I don't want to leave it until I have to.

There are many farms, and mansions, and castles, in various parts of the world, which have been in the possession of the same family for several generations. Even in the cities there are real-estate holdings which have passed from grandfather to grandson, with their "unearned increment." Yet the Astors do not live where they used to live; and the Croyes, who claim to be the most ancient princely house of the world, cannot afford to inhabit their castles without American subsidy. The Hohenzollerns and the Hapsburgs have had a notorious moving. But I fancy they sometimes hanker for their former dwellings.

At a banquet in New York or Chicago or Los Angeles or San Francisco, how many men do you meet who were born in those cities? At a mass-meeting how many of the shouters can say

"My foot is on my native heath"?

MOVING DAY

If we could have a plebiscite of the world on the proposition: *We claim the right to stay where we are and we promise never to move:* how many affirmative votes do you suppose you would get? Would it make any difference whether people were living in private homes or socialistic phalansteries? Would not every individual regard "an habitation enforced" as a kind of prison?

How many times have you moved, reader? For myself, including childhood, the number runs up to ten times, not counting a half-dozen summer cottages in which my family has been installed, and a villa in Switzerland, a house in Paris, a hut in Norway, and a mansion in The Hague. None of them has made much difference in the real values of life. Things look rather settled for me now, with a winter camp in New Jersey and a summer shack on the Maine coast. In both of these temporary homes work is pleasant, and in either of them I should be happy to labor through to the end of the job. But I will not accept a guaranty of that desired fate on condition of a pledge to undertake no more travels, no more adventures.

I have been thinking of the "moving" episodes of some of the writers whom I love most to read.

CAMP-FIRES

Shakespeare, after many mutations, settled down as a rich man in the best house at Stratford-on-Avon; but he had to leave it in less than five years. Milton was forced to many changes of residence, and at the end he was a poor man, and cared not much where he lived, provided he could have music and the joy of inward vision. Burns was an inspired migratory crofter; Wordsworth, a footpath adventurer, who nested finally at Rydal Mount. Charles Lamb was never driven from London and the "sweet security" of city streets, but he complained charmingly of the inconvenience of moving his abode within those precincts. Tennyson in youth moved often, but when the time came he fixed his winter home at Farringford and his summer home at Aldworth. Browning belonged to London and to Italy, and moved around as it pleased him, always pursuing his dramatic quest of the individual soul. Dickens and Thackeray were Londoners indubitable, but they shifted residences often within their city, and they travelled abroad, and they searched for a general human view of life. Stevenson was by choice and by necessity an adventurer; how many "movings" he had between Edinburgh and Samoa I know not; but through them all he

MOVING DAY

followed his dream of telling vivid stories of life, and of making true comments upon it in his essays. Kipling is still with us in the modern "movies," so we may not speak of him without reserve. We know that he has had habitations in India, in Vermont, and in Sussex, and that whether he lives in Bombay or in Burwash he keeps with him the same keen vision, straight word, and what Mrs. Gerould calls his "remarkable rightness." But, if I mistake not, his movings have carried him far beyond his first "Plain Tales from the Hills."

After all, reader, be we rich or poor, learned or unlearned, is not Moving Day marked in all our calendars? Is it not a symbol of the unexempt condition of our mortal pilgrimage?

From house to house we move; but that signifies little, if we do not overburden ourselves with rubbish.

From youth to age we move; but that is not fatal if we do not overload ourselves with prejudices.

From opinion to opinion we move; but that is natural if we are not forced to do it in haste. The man who thinks when old precisely the same on all points as he thought when young, is not a conservative. He is an obstacle.

CAMP-FIRES

I recall what Stevenson says in one of his essays: "I look back to the time when I was a Socialist with something like regret. I have convinced myself (for the moment) that we had better leave these great changes to what we call great blind forces; their blindness being so much more perspicacious than the little, peering, partial eyesight of men. I seem to see that my own scheme would not answer; and all the other schemes I have ever heard propounded would depress some elements of goodness just as much as they would encourage others."

Schemes, theories, systems and panaceas are the lambrequins and antimacassars of the mental life,—things to be left behind on Moving Day. They will not fit the new house. Only the essentials are worth transportation.

For my part, there are just three things that seem worth carrying through all earthly migrations of the spirit. First, the Ten Commandments. Second, the Golden Rule. Third, the "faithful saying, and worthy of all acceptation, that Christ Jesus came into the world to save sinners."

Among the typically transient dwellings of the world are the parsonage, the residence of the mili-

Is not moving day-marked in all our calendars?

MOVING DAY

tary or naval commandant, and the White House at Washington.

Do you remember the inscription that George Herbert wrote for the mantelpiece of his vicarage in Bemerton?

"TO MY SUCCESSOR
"If thou chance for to find
A new house to thy mind,
And built without thy cost;
Be good to the poor,
As God gives thee store,
And then my labor's not lost."

But the symbol of Moving Day runs far beyond the earthly mutations of dwelling, and the changes of opinion and theory, to which we are all subject. It reminds us of the great migration from the known to the unknown, which we call death.

Here is something universal, inevitable, and therefore worth thinking about. This is Moving Day, indeed. Not one of us can get away from it when it comes.

Yet I have no sympathy with those who would make the fact of death the controlling factor of life. The flaming inscriptions on the bill-boards, "Prepare to meet thy God," and the exhortations of the preachers, "Live to-day as if you were to die to-morrow," leave me cold. The meeting, (I say it reverently,) has already taken place. I do not expect to die to-morrow. I want to take life as it comes,—as bravely, as decently, as cheerfully as possible. There are lots of innocent, interesting, and possibly useful things which I propose doing to-day, which I should probably not do if I thought that I had to die to-morrow.

The beloved ones, the friends, who have moved before me into the unknown world, I believe are still living. I have no need of Sir Oliver Lodge nor of the excessively Belgian Shakespeare, Maeterlinck, to assure me of their existence. I rely upon a better Teacher.

Nor do I think that my invisible friends would choose to speak to me through persons,—mediums, —with whom they would have had no sympathy nor intercourse in mortal life. Nor would they use a patented *Ouija* board for their communications. They would speak to me directly,—my father, my dear daughter Dorothea,—and I believe they have done so, whether in the body or out of the body, I know not. But these are "things which it is not lawful for a man to utter."

MOVING DAY

Meanwhile let us take our earthly moving days as best we can. And for the last migration a word from Joseph Beaumont, written three centuries ago, is still timely:

> "Home is everywhere to thee
> Who canst thine own dwelling be;
> Yea, tho' ruthless Death assail thee,
> Still thy lodging will not fail thee:
> Still thy Soul's thine own; and she
> To an House removed shall be;
> An eternal House above,
> Walled, and roofed, and paved with Love.
> There shall these mud-walls of thine,
> Gallantly repaired, out-shine
> Mortal stars;—no stars shall be
> In that Heaven but such as Thee."

VIII

FIRELIGHT VIEWS

CIVILIZATION began with a wood-fire.

'Tis the coal-fire that has carried it on,—and, some think, too far.

The warmth diffused by burning wood is assuredly the oldest of "creature comforts." Doubtless Adam and Eve knew the joy of it when they started from Eden on the long adventure. The nights are sometimes biting cold in Mesopotamia, however hot the days, and the gentle calefaction of a few blazing sticks must have been grateful to the shivering pair,—especially in the fig-leafy period of their attire, before they had received the heavenly gift of fur coats.

Certainly their great-grandson Jubal, "the father of all such as handle the harp and the organ," and his half-brother Tubal-Cain, "the instructer of every artificer in brass and iron," had fires of wood, perhaps also of charcoal, for their work. And so, or in some such fashion, all human arts and crafts, inventions and contrivances, have sprung from the red seed of fire, planted in the bodies of trees, the ancient friends of man.

FIRELIGHT VIEWS

Greek poetry tells the same tale otherwise. Prometheus, the foresighted, stole a spark from the hearth of the great hall of Olympus, and brought it to earth hidden in a stalk of fennel. For this the jealous Olympians were enraged at him, and condemned him to undying torture.

But the tribes of the Orient say that the benevolent fire-thief was a bird; and the North American Indians hold that it was a coyote,—a beast which has kept the trick of theft, without a trace of benevolence.

Tell the tale as you will, the meaning is identical. It was the mastery of fire that gave man the advantage over the lower animals in all material things. It built Memphis, Nineveh, Babylon, Jerusalem, Athens, Rome, and many other cities of renown. But in the beginning, and through innumerable centuries thereafter, it was only and always *woodfire*.

Possibly, now and then petroleum was added (after the manner of the rash and indolent housemaid) to hasten and augment the blaze. Does not Job, that early capitalist, boast that "the rocks poured me out rivers of oil"?

But the amorphous mineral, coal,—the mummy

of wood,—the latent heat of fallen forests laid up in cold storage for our use,—who can tell when it was first discovered? At what time and by what chance, happy or unhappy, did man find out that those dusky rocks would burn?

Was it when some cave-dweller made his fire-place on a vein of lignite passing through the floor of his den, and suddenly saw it all aglow? Was it when some primitive cottager took a fancy to those smooth blocks of black stone for the building of his hearth, and found that his fire laid hold upon its foundations? In cave or cottage, that must have been a surprise. No doubt the news of it spread quickly as a dire portent. Perhaps the legends of fire-and-smoke-breathing dragons, inhabiting caverns among the hills, had their source in some such accident.

Be that as it may, it is certain that the use of coal for heating purposes was late to begin and slow to progress. The British apparently led the way, somewhere in the twelfth century, and by the sixteenth century the practice had so increased in London that the Brewers Company petitioned Queen Elizabeth to forbid it, alleging "Hersealfe greatley greved and anoyed with the taste and

FIRELIGHT VIEWS

smoke of the sea cooles." In Paris it went the same way. The dainty Parisians maintained that the burning of coal poisoned the air, dirtied the wash, injured the lungs, and spoiled the complexion of the ladies. Horrible! This barbarous practice must terminate itself. Accordingly it was forbidden in 1714, and again as late as 1769.

Yet somehow or other it continued, and grew, and spread upon the face of earth, and diffused its sulphurous fumes in air, piling above our monstrous cities what Ruskin has called the "storm-cloud of the nineteenth century." Tall chimneys, vomiting gloom, broke the sky-line. Forges blazed and flared. Factories sprang like exhalations from the ground. Railway-trains ran roaring up and down the continents. Steamships wove their spider-web of crossing lines and lanes over the sea. Man's power to make things and to move things increased tenfold, a hundredfold, a thousandfold. And of this new world,—civilized, we call it,—coal-fire is king.

For this reason, some say, Germany attacked France in 1870 to gain possession of the coal-fields of Lorraine, and again in 1914 to grab the Briey Basin and the mines around Lens. For this reason, some say, the empire of Britain is founded on a coal-pit, and when that is exhausted it will fall. For this reason, some say, the present prosperity of mankind is illusory and transient, and some coalless day we shall all freeze or starve to death. An imitator of Rudyard Kipling puts it thus:

When the ultimate coal-mine is empty and the miners' last labor is done,
When the pick and the drill are silent and the furnaces die, one by one,
Then the trains will stall on the railway, and the factories all grow dumb,
And shivering man will cover his head and wait for The End to come.

Perhaps,—perhaps! Yet the prophecy does not curdle my marrow. As the Kingship of Coal was not primeval, so its perpetuity is not assured. Nor would the dethronement of the present monarch necessarily be final and fatal. A competent Regent has been discovered in Oil. Behind him, like a sturdy heir-apparent, we see the rising head of Electric Power. In the dim distance we discern various heirs presumptive,—Sun-heat yet unexploited; Tide-force yet unharnessed. That embryonic wonder, of whom Sir Oliver Lodge tells us, Atomic Explosion, still slumbers in the womb

FIRELIGHT VIEWS

of nature, waiting the day of delivery. Who knows but what The Coming Man, having taken the needful precautions, may gently insert a spoonful of atoms into a safety-exploder and generate power enough to run the world's machines for a year?

Meantime there is no present reason, moral or economic, why we should not come back, after our day's work, and sit down beside the old wood-fire, and get the good of it.

Once a power, it is still a friend. With a moderate and variable heat, it gives out light and cheer. It talks a little, and sings a little, and makes a solitary room less lonely. Old-fashioned it certainly is; wasteful it may be,—extravagant, if you like to call it so, with fire-wood at its present price; but for me it answers precisely to the French philosopher's definition of a luxury,—*chose très nécessaire*.

Indeed it is the last of the luxuries that I would forego under duress of the High Cost of Living. If need be, as the poet says,

> I can do without sugar and butter and eggs;
> I can give up my carriage and trust to my legs;
> The dream of a motor, or even a Ford

CAMP-FIRES

I renounce, while my plumber rolls by like a lord;
I can cut out my tailor, and wear my old shoes,
And resign from the club to escape the high dues;
I abstain from the movie, the opera, the play,
The lure of the bookshop, the florist's display;
All, all, I surrender that Hard Times require;
But leave me, ah leave me, my bonny wood-fire.

My fireplace is not a splendiferous one, with huge, carven mantel, brought (or copied) from some Italian palace or Bavarian castle. I like not these gigantic intruders in modest American rooms. The fire smokes or smoulders discouraged in their cavernous depths. A plain, useful hearth, by preference of red bricks or tiles, and a chimney that draws well, are worth more than all the decorated chimneypieces in the world.

In andirons I would admit a little fancy, but no ostentation. Mine are twin near-bronze figures of Indian maidens that used to stand, long ago, on top of the newel-posts at the foot of the stairway in an ancient New York hostelry. These I found by chance in a junk-shop, and had low steel bars fitted to them, to hold the wood. Goldilocks calls them Pocahontas and Minnehaha. They are not beautiful, nor ugly, but they seem to fit the place,

In andirons I would admit a little fancy.

FIRELIGHT VIEWS

smiling as they warm their backs at the blaze. They appear to be dressed, let me hasten to say, in decorous deerskin garments with fringes.

Behind these proper and benignant figures the fire is kindled every morning from the first of October to the first of May, and later if need be. Is the day warm? The windows are easily opened. Is it bitter cold? Then pile on the wood,—as Horace says,

> *"Dissolve frigus, ligna super foco*
> *Large reponens."*

That is, in modern American, beat the cold by boosting the fire.

Do you want to know how to light it? I can tell you a trick that is worth learning in these days of costly kindling.

You must have a thick bed of ashes. This is difficult to secure and protect if you are married. But it can be done by making concessions on other points. Now pull out your fire-dogs a little and put the round backlog behind them, resting on the ashes. Stuff a few sheets of dry newspaper, (old copies of the *Social Uplifter* are best,) under its curving side. Above this place just four,—no more, —sticks of kindling-wood, not horizontally, mind you, but perpendicularly, or rather "slantendicularly," leaning against the backlog. In front of this, lying on the andirons and close against the kindlings, place your forelog. Then apply the match to the paper. In two minutes you will have a beautiful little blaze. Now you can lay on your third log,—but gently, gently,—and your fire is well started for the day.

Reader, you may think that paragraph meticulous and trifling. But really and truly it is an invaluable guide-post. If you will follow it, in a year it will save you the price of a subscription to the magazine, to say nothing of the profanity which you would have expended in trying to light *choked fires*. If your wife won't let you have the bed of ashes, try that excellent invention, the Cape Cod Firelighter.

Air is the great thing, remember,—free circulation, a good draft,—both for fire-building and for thought-kindling. We smother our poor minds by piling on ideas and theories. We choke our high-school and college education with a preposterous overload of "courses." We encumber our social programme with vast heaps of universal reform, and complain that "we can't get anything done,"

FIRELIGHT VIEWS

because we fail in the fool's effort to do everything at once.

Why try to do good things in a silly way? Why waste matches by applying them immediately to the backlog? Take the little sticks first. And above all let the fresh air of open discussion, practical experiment, illustration, comparison of experiences, criticism, humor, and enthusiasm play freely through the fire of your theories and plans.

In education, for example, I would sweep away half of the "courses" and two-thirds of the "examinations," and concentrate attention on teaching boys and girls to use their powers of observation accurately, their powers of reasoning intelligently, their powers of imagination and sympathy vividly, and their powers of will sanely and strongly,—in short, to know things as they are, to conceive them as they might be, and to help make them as they ought to be. That is the real purpose of education. And I think it may be reached, or at least approached, better through a few studies well chosen than through a mass of studies piled on at random.

But these are only "firelight views," reader; they are not systematic, sharp-cut, unalterable theories. To such the magical light of the dancing, flickering flames, the mystical glow of the orange-red embers, are not favorable. They lend themselves rather to the inspiration of dreams, and hopes, and fancies. They are friendly to memories and visions, without which indeed the journey of life would be dull and cheerless.

Yet I cannot agree with that good British essayist, E. V. Lucas, when he suggests that the wood-fire harmonizes with spiritualistic experiments, and goes on to say, "If England were warmed wholly by hot-water pipes or gas-stoves, the Society for Psychical Research would soon be dissolved." On the contrary it is precisely in that stale-heated, stuffy, musky atmosphere that mediums flourish and perform their most marvellous feats with their feet. The frankly blazing wood-fire is too healthy for them.

I have heard of only one successful *séance* that was held beside an open hearth. The story was told me by the Reverend Doctor Wonderman, a delightful comrade and a firm believer. He was sitting with a mediumistic couple, and they had produced for his benefit during the evening various "manifestations" of knocks and scratchings and movements of furniture. The "control" was sup-

FIRELIGHT VIEWS

posed to be the soul of a departed Indian Chief,—Bumbagoostook, or some such name as that,—a penetrating spirit, but wayward, and of rude, boisterous humor. As a final and conclusive proof the Doctor asked that Bumbagoostook should hand him his favorite pipe, which was then lying on the mantelpiece. Instantly the pipe leaped from the shelf, hurtled through the air, and struck the good Doctor violently in the midriff. Whether he laughed or not, I do not know, but it seems to me likely. Nothing of that kind has ever happened by my wood-fire. I prefer to get my pipes for myself, rather than have to do with unrefined spirits.

Plenty of good things have been written about wood-fires,—whole books, in fact, like Hamilton Mabie's "My Study Fire," and Charles Dudley Warner's "Backlog Studies." There are also little fragments scattered here and there, which are worth picking up and remembering.

Horace has an excellent bit in his second epode, where he describes the honest farmer's wife,—modest, merry, sunburned woman, glad to play her part in keeping house and bearing children,—who lays the dry fagots on the hearth, ready to welcome the homecoming of her tired husband.

CAMP-FIRES

Cicero in his dialogue "*De Senectute*" gives a graphic picture of old Manius Curius sitting quietly by his country fireside and refusing the conquered Samnites who brought him a heap of gold. He said that he did not think it as fine to have gold as to be superior to those who had it.

Tibullus, the so-called bucolic poet, breathes a true fireside wish in his first elegy:

> "Let lowly fortune lead my life
> In quiet ways, remote from strife,
> If only on this hearth of mine
> A constant fire may brightly shine."

But there is nothing better on this subject than the lines of Robert Messinger, an American, writing on the familiar theme of "old wine, old wood, old books, and old friends." Here is the second stanza:

> "Old wood to burn!
> Ay, bring the hill-side beech
> From where the owlets meet and screech
> And ravens croak;
> The crackling pine, and cedar sweet;
> Bring too a lump of fragrant peat,
> Dug 'neath the fern;
> The knotted oak;

FIRELIGHT VIEWS

A fagot too, perhap,
Whose bright flame dancing, winking,
Shall light us at our drinking;
    While the oozing sap
Shall make sweet music to our thinking."

At our place in Maine I have always been able to keep the home-fires burning with white birch and dry spruce from our own woodlands around the bungalow. But that is quite a different thing from feeding the hearth with fuel from the eight acres of home-lot here in Princeton.

Every now and then one of the trees that my own hands have planted and tended here is smitten in its lusty youth and must come down; and sometimes there are deaths among the older trees, and they are brought to the funeral pyre. From such sad events I draw what comfort I can, and remember by the hearth the joy that the trees gave while they were living.

There was a pair of silver cut-leaf birches that succumbed one after the other, to some mysterious malady; a massy rock-maple that grew too great and blocked the sunlight from the windows; a trio of tall Norway firs that died at the top; some cherry-trees fallen into barren decrepitude, and mulberries

CAMP-FIRES

rent and crippled beyond repair by a beautiful, cruel ice-storm. Once a giant pine-tree was struck by lightning, and we gave him a splendid, long-drawn flame-burial, with rattling, crackling accompaniments, like salvoes of musketry over the ashes of a fallen hero. Once there was the remnant of an ancient orchard that went the way of all wood and passed into fire. That was the best of all.

Old apple-wood burns cleanly, brightly, serenely, with a delicate and spicy fragrance. The flames bloom softly over the logs; they play around them and dance above them with shifting colors of canary yellow, and pale blue, and saffron; they send up wavering pennons of pure golden light, which sink down again into fringes of mellow radiance. Deeper and deeper the transforming element sinks into the heart of the log, which still keeps its shape, an incandescent round, silvered with a fine white ash; until at last the stick breaks and crumbles into glowing coals, of a color which no words can describe. It is like the petals of a certain rose, whose tint I remember, but whose name I have forgotten. (Tell me its name, reader, if you are sending a letter this way.) So the lovely ruins of the old apple-tree lie heaped upon the hearth, and over them flow

FIRELIGHT VIEWS

tiny ripples of azure and mauve and violet flame, lower and lower, fainter and fainter, till all dies down into gray, and the tree has rendered its last offering of beauty and service to man.

One of the practical merits of an open wood-fire is its convenience for destroying rubbish. Old pamphlets and letters, dusty manuscripts that you once thought would be worth touching up for publication, scraps and fragments of all kinds that have cluttered your shelves and drawers for years, even new books that you have tried in vain to read, —how easy it is to drop them into the blaze and press them down with the poker!

But the habit is a bad one, for three reasons: first, because it dishonors the hearth with black ashes; second, because you may set the chimney on fire; third, because you never can tell what *is* rubbish.

You remember how King Jehoiakim made a mistake in that respect when Jehudi came into his presence to read from a little manuscript an extremely disagreeable prophecy of Jeremiah. There was a fire on the hearth burning before him. And it came to pass, that when Jehudi had read three or four leaves, he cut it with the penknife and cast it into

CAMP-FIRES

the fire. "So," thought the king, "we have done with that rubbish." But neither was it rubbish nor had he done with it. For Jeremiah caused another little roll to be written with the same unpleasant words in it, and there were added unto them many like words, and they were all true, and it was worse for Jehoiakim in the end than if he had preserved and heeded the first book.

Many a man burns what he wishes later he had kept.

Another use of a wood-fire, though you can hardly call it a practical one, is its power of begetting fantasies, some romantic and some grotesque, in the mind of him that gazeth into it.

Here I often sit, when the day's task is done, and indulge my vagrant fancy with improbable adventures and impossible labors. To go a-hunting in the Caucasus, and a-fishing in New Zealand; to complete either my long-planned book on "Wild Animals that Have Refused to Meet Me," or that much-needed treatise on "The Moral Effects of Chewing Gum"; to get out a serious edition of *The New Republic*,—think what it would mean to the world if that journal, with all its natural gifts of omniscience, omnipresence, and omnipotence, only

FIRELIGHT VIEWS

had the added grace of ethical earnestness! But these are vain visions. Let us return to the realities.

The very best thing about a real wood-fire is its power of drawing friends around it. Here comes the new Herodotus, not to discuss the problems of antiquity which he has already settled, but to tell the most absorbing tales and anecdotes of the people that you know or have known, and to dispute your most cherished opinions in a way that makes you love him. Here comes Fra Paolo, the happy controversialist, ready for a friendly bicker on any subject under heaven, and full of projects for rescuing the most maligned characters of history. Here come the lean young Literary Rancher with tales of the once wild West, and the wonderful Writer of Sad Stories, who is herself always cheerful. Here come Goldilocks and Brownie to sit on the rug, tuck up their skirts and toast their shins, while they talk of their joyous plans and propound deep simple questions that no one can answer. Here come travellers and professors and poets and ambassadors, not reserved and stately, but thawed and relaxed to a delightful companionship by the magic of the wood-fire.

Well, they have all gone their way now, and while

CAMP-FIRES

the logs burn down, I sit alone in the book-room, pencilling these lines. But you, reader,—if your eyes glance over them at all, it will be in the happy season when your fire is kindled out-of-doors. In the deep, green woods, on the mountainside, by the seashore, on the bank of some quiet lake or flowing stream;—"the camp-fire, the cooking-fire, the smudge-fire, the little friendship-fire";—but that is an old story, of which I have written in another book. I will not repeat it now, though the theme is one upon which I could play new variations forever. Let me rather wish you good luck in the lighting of your fire in the open, and leave with you a saying from old Plutarch.

He says (in his *Symposiacs*, Question IV,) that when his guests have departed he would leave one flame burning as a symbol of his reverence for fire. No other thing is so like a creature alive. It is moved and nourished from within; and by its brightness, like the soul, reveals and illuminates things around it; and even in dying resembles a vital principle, sighing and trembling ere it departs.

This, then, is what the Greek philosopher has to say about the firelight. But he says it, mark you, only of fire indoors.

FIRELIGHT VIEWS

Outdoors the case is different. There the fire, though lovelier, must never be left alone. Fold your tents and march on; but first put out the embers, lest a single spark, running wild in the woods, make you the careless father of a great conflagration.

IX

FISHING IN STRANGE WATERS

For half a year, now, I have been writing a paper a month, without so much as mentioning a subject near to my heart,—the ancient, apostolic, consolatory art of angling.

It must be admitted the season has not been in harmony with that subject. It has been a villainous rude winter, (1919–20,) violent, pitiless, persistent as a Prussian; ice on top of snow and snow on top of ice, and howling ravenous winds, so that even those hardened anglers who let down their lines through holes in frozen ponds, have been debarred from their gelid sport and driven to find comfort by the fireside.

Yet fancy does not freeze in zero weather. Memories and dreams run out across the cold to leafy forests and flowing rivers and sparkling lakes. If there has been thus far no word of angling in these essays, you may set it down, reader, to a self-denying ordinance, and reward me with leave to tell a few stories of fishing. Not fish-stories, mark you;

FISHING IN STRANGE WATERS

for I have no great catches, no finny monsters to describe; only a few small experiences which may serve to illustrate the spirit of the game.

For such recital the signal has been given. Last week, on a sharp icicled morning, the first hoarse robin bravely sounded his *tup-tup-tup* outside my window. When these pages come to you the greenwood tree will be full of song and the kingfisher flashing blue along the stream.

In many strange waters have I fished, the Nile and the Jordan, the Rhine, the Rhone, and the Danube, but in none that seemed to me so strange as the little rivers where I cast an occasional fly while the world-war was going on.

I was sent to Holland, (presumably "for my country's good,") in the autumn of 1913. There was no fishing there to speak of. Canals, slow-moving rivers, shallow lakes, with their store of pike and perch and eels, offer no attraction to a sporting angler. To catch such fish is more a business than a sport. There was one pretty trout-stream in South Limburg; but it was so beset with factories and mills and persecuted by bait-fishermen and netters that it did not tempt me

CAMP-FIRES

In these sad circumstances of deprivation, it seemed "*almost* Providential" to find that the American Minister to the Netherlands was also accredited to the Grand Duchy of Luxembourg. A strict sense of official duty called him thither every year; and a willingness to enjoy small gifts of pleasure paid him wages by the way.

Nature has been kind to that little inland country, and history has handled it roughly enough to make it picturesque with human interest. It holds more castles ruined and unrestored than any other land of equal size. Its small triangle of territory,—about a thousand square miles, dovetailed in between Germany, France, and Belgium,—lies on top of the Ardennes, a thousand feet or more above sea-level. It is furrowed by deep valleys, clothed with rich woods of beech and pine, diversified with gray and red cliffs, embroidered with wild flowers and many bright unnavigable rivers. Its royal family contains the six loveliest young princesses in the world; and its 250,000 people are as friendly, hospitable, and independent as the traveller's heart could wish. All this and more you may find set forth admirably in the big book on *Luxembourg* by Mr. George Renwick, the British war correspondent.

FISHING IN STRANGE WATERS

For useful information I refer you to him, and turn to my fishing.

My first excursion was made in June, 1914,—the Potsdam Plotters' month. Of what I saw then to convince me that Germany had chosen war and was ready to force it, the story is told in *Fighting for Peace* and need not be repeated.

The second trip was in April, 1915, after Germany's long crime had been begun. It was necessary for the American Minister to go down to take charge of certain British interests in Luxembourg,—a few poor people who had been stranded there and who sorely needed money and help. (What a damned inhuman thing war is, no one knows who has not been in the midst of it!) Mr. Derulle, the faithful American Consular Agent in the city of Luxembourg, did the work, but the minister had to convey the funds and supervise the accounts.

The journey was interesting. The German Minister at The Hague was most polite and obliging in the matter of providing a *visé* for the passports, and giving the needful papers with big seals to pass the guards in what was euphemistically called "German-occupied territory." It grated on my nerves, but it was the only way.

CAMP-FIRES

"Which route would you prefer to have me follow," I asked, "through Germany, or through Belgium?"

"But, my dear colleague," replied the courteous Baron von Kühlman, "that is entirely for you to choose."

"With your advice," I answered, "since I am asking a favor."

"Well, then," he smiled, "probably you would like to go by way of Maestricht and Aix-la-Chapelle, —in your own automobile,—we will detail an escort to make the journey easier and quicker."

At the border-barrier,—a double fence of electrically charged barbed wire, with a sentried opening ten feet wide,—the escort appeared. He was an amiable and intelligent captain of cavalry in the German reserve, university graduate, cloth manufacturer, father of a family, pleasant companion, named von M———. His conversation was good. Three of his remarks were memorable because they lifted a corner of the veil from the German state of mind.

We were rolling along the splendid highway south from Aix, through a country bare of men not in uniform. "This is a terrible war," exclaimed the

FISHING IN STRANGE WATERS

captain, "not our fault, but terrible for us, all the same! Do you think a quiet middle-aged man like me enjoys being called away from his business, his home, his children, to join the colors? We shall be ruined. Of course we shall win; but what? Our money spent, our industries crippled, the best of our youth killed or maimed,—it is a bad outlook, but we are forced to accept it."

In the quaint timbered villages on the plateau of the *Hohes Venn* many soldiers were on furlough, strolling with the village girls in frankly amatory attitudes. "Pleasant for these boys to come home for a few days and see their old sweethearts again," I remarked. The captain smiled: "Yes,—well,—but,—you see, these boys don't belong to these villages; and the girls are not old sweethearts, you see. But the army does not discourage it. Men will be needed. They will all be good Germans."

Just before we cross the border beyond St. Vith the captain says: "My general at Aix has telegraphed the German commandant in Luxembourg to detail an officer to act as escort and body-guard to your Excellency in that country." Polite, but astounding!

"Many thanks," I answered, "most thoughtful

of the general. But it will not be necessary. In Luxembourg I shall be under protection of her Royal Highness the Grand Duchess, sovereign of an independent state, in which the Germans have volunteered to guard the railways. After paying my respects to her and to the Prime Minister, I shall call on the German commandant to assure him that no escort is desired. Will that be correct according to your theory?"

The captain blinked, looked down at his boots, then grinned approvingly. "Absolutely correct," he said, "that is just our theory. But, *Gott im Himmel*, you Americans go straight to the point!"

All the diplomatic affairs of the next ten days went smoothly; and there were three celestial days on various streams, the details of which are vague in memory, but the bright spots shine out.

One day was passed with my friend the notary Charles Klein, of the old town of *Wiltz*, a reputable lawyer and a renowned, impassioned fisher. He led us, with many halts for refreshment at wayside inns, to the little river *Sure*, which runs through a deep, flowery vale from west to east, across the Grand Duchy.

Our stretch of water was between the high-arched

FISHING IN STRANGE WATERS

Pont de Misère and the abandoned slate-quarry of *Bigonville*. The stream was clear and lively, with many rapids but no falls. It was about the size of the Neversink below Claryville, but more open. The woods crept down the steep, enfolding hills, now on this side, now on that, but never on both. One bank was always open for long casting, which is a delight. The brown trout, (*salmo fario*), were plentiful and plump, running from a quarter of a pound to a pound weight. Larger ones there must have been, but we did not see them. They accepted our tiny American flies,—Beaverkill, Cahill, Queen of the Water, Royal Coachman, and so on,— at par value, without discount for exchange. It was easy, but not too easy, to fill our creels.

My son and comrade Tertius agreed with me that the European brown trout, though distinctly less comely than the American brook-trout, or the "rainbow" of the Pacific Coast, (not to speak of the gorgeous *salmo Rooservelti* of Volcano Creek), is a fine fellow, a "dead game sport." The birds that fluttered and skipped and sang around us were something of a puzzle to Tertius, who is an expert on this subject in his own country. Some of them, —blackbirds, wrens, tomtits, linnets, swallows, and so on,—were easy to identify. The crow and the kingfisher are pretty much the same everywhere. But there were also many strangers.

"It is funny," said he, "I can't tell their names, but I understand their language perfectly."

Philip Gilbert Hamerton in *The Sylvan Year* says that there is a tradition among the peasants of the *Val Sainte Véronique* that every bird repeats a phrase of its own in French words, and that some wise old persons have the gift of understanding them. This gift must be kept secret till a man comes to die; then he may communicate it to one of his family. But the trouble is that when a man is on his death-bed, he is usually thinking about other things than bird-lore. So the gift fades out, say the peasants, and may soon be lost, like other wonderful things.

The second day of this series that I remember clearly was spent on a smaller stream, north of the *Sure*, with Mr. Le G., the son of the British Consul, and other pleasant companions. The name of the stream is forgotten, but the clear water and the pleasant banks of it are "in my mind's eye, Horatio." It was a meadow-brook very like one that I know not far from Norfolk, Connecticut, whither

FISHING IN STRANGE WATERS

I have often gone to fish with my good friend the village storekeeper, S. Cone.

Now there is in all the world no water more pleasant to fish than a meadow-brook, provided the trout are there. The casting is easy, the wading is light, the fish are fat, the flowers of the field are plenteous, and the birds are abundant and songful. We filled our baskets, dined at the wayside inn, a jolly company, and motored back by moonlight to the city of Luxembourg.

Concerning the 1916 journey to my outlying post there are a few notes in my diary. I travelled in May by rail through Cologne and Gerolstein and Trier. There was no visible escort; but probably there was one unseen; for at every place where I had to change trains, somebody was waiting for me, and a compartment was reserved. Everything was orderly and polite, even in the stations where hundreds of thousands of green-gray soldiers were rushing on their way to the great battle at *Verdun*. (Perhaps it was because I spoke German that people were so courteous. Yet for that very reason no one could have mistaken me for a native.) But the war-bread in the dining-cars was dreadful: butter and sugar were not at all: and the meat, such as it was, had already done duty in the soup.

At Gerolstein, (name made dear by Offenbach's *Grande Duchesse*,) many civilians got into the train with guns, green hats, and netted game-bags with fringes.

"What go they to shoot," I asked a neighbor, "is it not the closed time?"

"But not for crows," he replied.

"Crows!" I cried, with a sickening thought of the near battle-fields.

"Yes, *mein Herr*, crows are good to eat, healthy food. In all the meat-shops are they to buy."

In the capital of Luxembourg, perched on its high rock, the German garrison was still in evidence, tramping in stolid troops through the streets while the citizens turned their backs. Not even a small boy would run after the soldiers: think what that means! No longer did the field-gray ones sing when they marched, as they used to do in 1915. They plodded silent, evidently depressed. The war which they had begun so gayly was sinking into their souls. The first shadows of the Great Fatigue were falling upon them; but lightly as yet.

Once I thought I heard a military band playing

FISHING IN STRANGE WATERS

"God Save the King." I ran to the balcony, but turned back again, remembering that the same tune is set to "*Heil Dir im Siegerkranz.*"

The Grand Duchess was already away at her summer castle of Colmar-Berg. So after "posing" the needful cards and writing my name in the book at the old palace, and finishing three days of official business (and luncheons) with Prime Minister Thorn and other dignitaries, I was free to turn to the streams.

The first excursion was with Mr. Emile Meyrisch, a genial, broad-shouldered ironmaster, the head of great forges at Esch, Diffeedange, and Petange in the south country, and an angler of the most confirmed sect. In politics he was a liberal, in business perhaps rather an autocrat, and in practice a friend to his employees, looking carefully after their food-supply and running an open-air school on a hilltop for their children, to keep them well and strong.

He took me to the valley of the *Clerf*, the loveliest little river in Luxembourg. By ruined castles and picturesque villages, among high-shouldered hills and smooth green meadows and hanging woods it runs with dancing ripples, long curves, and eddying pools where the trout lurk close to the bank.

Its course is not from west to east, like the *Sure*, (no, I will *not* call it by that common German name the *Sauer*.) The *Clerf* runs from north to south. I suppose that was why the south wind, on that quiet sunny morning, carried into the placid valley a strange continuous rumbling like very distant thunder. But the clear stream paid no heed to it, flowing with soft, untroubled whispers of contentment on its winding way. And the birds were not dismayed nor hindered in their musical love-making. And the flowers bloomed in bright peacefulness, neither dimmed nor shaken by that faint vibration of the upper air. Undoubtedly it was the noise of the guns in the offensive Crown Prince's "Great Offensive" at *Verdun*, a hundred kilometres away.

Strange that a sound could travel so far! Dreadful to think what it meant! It crossed the beauty of the day. But what could one do? Only fish on, and wait, and work quietly for a better day when America should come into the war and help to end it right.

A very fat and red-faced Major, whom I had met before at *Clervaux*, rode by in a bridle-path through the meadow. He stopped to salute and exchange greetings.

FISHING IN STRANGE WATERS

"How goes it?" I asked.

"*Verdammt schlecht,*" he replied. "This is a dull country. The people simply *won't* like us. I wish I was at home."

"I too!" I answered. "*Glückliche Reise!*"

We lunched in the roadside inn of *Wilwerwiltz;* a modest tavern, but a rich feast. The old river-guardian was there, a grizzled veteran who angled only with the fly, though his patrons were mostly bait-fishers. He had scorned to fish in the morning. But when he saw my basketful taken with the fly, his spirit was stirred within him, and he girded up his loins and went forth to the combat. That afternoon he beat my whole day's catch by three trout. He grinned as he laid his fish out in a long row on the bench in front of the inn.

I spent the night with Notary Klein at *Wiltz.* Ever hospitable, he made a little dinner for me at the *Hôtel du Commerce,*—a little dinner of many courses and rare vintages,—and like the bridegroom at Cana of Galilee he served the best wine last.

When we reached this point the notary presented a request. He said that three officers of the German garrison, who felt very lonely, had asked if they might come over to our table after dinner and

CAMP-FIRES

drink coffee with us. Had I any objection? Certainly not, if he had none. So they came, and we talked pleasantly for a couple of hours about various subjects. One of the officers was a professor of literature in a small German university. Both of the others were well-educated men. Finally we drifted toward the war.

'Why did America sell munitions only to the Allies? It was very unfair.'

'But the market was open to all. Doubtless anybody who had the money could buy.'

'Yes, perhaps; but then it was plain that if Germany bought them she could not get them home. It was most unfair, not truly neutral.'

'But could America be expected as a neutral to act so as to make up to Germany for her lack of effective sea-power?'

'No-o-o, perhaps not. But it was extremely unfair. No doubt those British-Americans who were so powerful in the United States were to blame for it.'

'On the contrary; Americans of German descent were most prominent in making munitions for the Allies. Take the name Schwab, for example, president of the Bethlehem Steel Company, a good Amer-

FISHING IN STRANGE WATERS

ican. Did the *Herren Offizieren* think his name was of British origin?'

Slight confusion and hearty laughter followed this question. Then the professor spoke up very gravely:

"There is one thing I should like to ask you, Excellency. You have travelled a good deal in this country. Have you heard the Luxembourgers make any objection to the conduct of the German army here?"

"None, *Herr Oberst*," I answered with equal gravity, "not the slightest! It is not the *conduct* of your soldiers to which Luxembourg objects, it is their *presence*."

"Well," he said smiling rather sadly, "God knows I am tired of it too. I want to go home to my books. But is there no chance that America will come finally to the help of Germany, her old friend?"

"Certainly," I replied, "there seems to be a very good chance. If the present submarine warfare continues, it is practically sure that America will assist Germany in the only possible way,—by creating a situation in which the war must come to an end. That would be the best conceivable help for Germany."

CAMP-FIRES

With this observation, (rather in the enigmatic style of the Delphic oracle,) and with an appropriate "good night," the conversation closed, and I went home with the Notary.

But the next day was not spent in fishing as we had planned. An invitation had come by telegraph during the night, bidding the American minister to lunch with the royal family at Colmar-Berg. The only available taxicab in Wiltz must be commandeered, and hot time made over the long road in order to reach the castle at the appointed hour.

"Punctuality," says the proverb, "is the courtesy due to kings"; and the saying has an extra, super-diplomatic force when the sovereign happens to be a very beautiful young lady.

Of the luncheon I will not write, since it was not official, though there were about thirty guests. Adhering to the old-fashioned rule, I hold that hospitality lays a certain restraint upon publicity. Yet there are some memories which may be recalled without offense.

The American minister's chair was at the right of the Grand Duchess, on whose delicate, sensitive face the strain of the last two years, and the sufferings of the poor among her people, had written thin

FISHING IN STRANGE WATERS

lines of care and grief. She had never coveted a crown,—nor did she wear one except a circlet of pearls in her dark hair,—and I am sure she was glad when the close of the war permitted her to hand over the reins of rulership to her sister Charlotte, with Luxembourg independent, sovereign, and free to follow her natural sympathies with France.

At my right was the little Duchess Antoinette. It was probably her first appearance at such a feast, for she was still a mere child, with her long hair loose on her shoulders. Her announced engagement to that hardened ruffian, the ex-Crown Prince of Bavaria, in 1918, was a shock to every one of decent feelings. Now that the German surrender under the form of armistice has put this horrid engagement, with other grisly things, into "innocuous desuetude," it is pleasant to recall and reflect upon the deliverance of the little Duchess from that royal incubus.

After all, royalties are flesh and blood. But there is a difference between the clean and the unclean, which no crown can disguise.

The day following the luncheon I had an early dinner with M. Pescatore, one of the ablest members of the Luxembourg Parliament, at his country house, and went out at sunset with Madame, to hunt the deer in a wonderful beech-forest along the valley of the *Mamer*.

She was a Belgian countess. Her hunting-dress made her look like Rosalind in the Forest of Arden, and she carried an effective little rifle. I took no gun, having passed the age when the killing of deer seems a pleasure. Hour after hour in the lingering twilight we roamed that enchanted woodland, among the smooth boles of the pillared beeches, under their high-arched roof of green, and treading lightly over the russet carpet of last year's fallen leaves. My spirited companion told me pitiful tales of things that she had seen, and knew by sure report from her relatives and friends in Belgium,—tales of the fierce and lewd realities of the German *Schrecklichkeit*,—things to make an honest man's blood hot within him.

Through the glimmering dusk, from thicket to thicket, the dim shapes of does and fawns flitted past us unharmed. Then a fine buck stood clearly outlined at the end of an open glade. The slender, eager huntress threw the rifle to her shoulder. A sharp crack echoed through the glade, and the buck

FISHING IN STRANGE WATERS

leaped away untouched. The huntress turned a half-disappointed face to me. "A bad shot," she said, "but I *could* shoot better than that. In Belgium, *par exemple*, with a Prussian boar for mark!"

My last day in Luxembourg was spent with Meyrisch on the upper waters of the *Sure*. Lovelier than ever seemed that merry, tranquil stream on that day of alternate showers and sunshine. The river-guardian who kept me company was a strapping young *Luxembourgeois* who had served as a volunteer in the French army and come home with a broken leg and an unbroken spirit. In the forenoon the record says that I took forty-two trout, in the afternoon thirteen. Late that night Meyrisch made a feast at the *Hôtel Brasseur* in Luxembourg. The landlord and his wife were of the company. Their oldest boy was with the Belgian army near *Ypres*. The final toast we drank was this: God protect the boy and the Cause he fights for!

Other fishing-days in war-time I recall. Two weeks in Norway in July, 1916, when I made acquaintance with the big salmon of the river Evanger, and proved the superiority of fly-fishing to the debased sport of "harling." Two days on the Itchen, near Winchester, just after I got out of hospital in

CAMP-FIRES

April, 1917, when my good friend G. E. M. Skues, secretary of the Fly-fishers' Club in London, showed me how to cast the dry fly so that two of those sophisticated Itchen trout were lured and landed. But I leave these things unchronicled, (having already run beyond the space assigned), and turn front-face and unabashed to meet and withstand the strictures of my severe and sour-complexioned reader, who has been following these lines with scornful impatience.

"Why," I hear him mutter, "does this foolish writer talk about silly things like fishing while the world-war was going on, and especially now that the great social problems of the New Era must be solved at once? He is a trifler, a hedonist, a man devoid of serious purpose and strenuous effort."

Well, friend, keep your bad opinion of me if it does you any good. Certainly it does me no harm.

I hold by the advice of the Divine Master who told His disciples to go a-fishing, and said to them when they were weary, "come ye yourselves apart into a desert place and rest awhile."

I remember the unconquerable French *poilus* whom I saw in their dugouts playing cards, and in the citadel of *Verdun* enjoying merry vaudeville

The ancient, apostolic, consolatory art of angling.

FISHING IN STRANGE WATERS

shows. I recall the soldiers whom I saw deliberately fishing on the banks of the *Marne* and the *Meuse* while the guns roared round us. I remember Theodore Roosevelt, (no slacker), who whenever the chance came rejoiced to go a-hunting, and to tell about it afterward. I believe that the most serious men are not the most solemn. I believe that a normal human being needs relaxation and pleasure to keep him from strained nerves and a temper of fanatical insanity.

I believe that the New Social State, whatever it may be, will not endure, nor be worth preserving, unless it has room within it for simple play, and pure fun, and uncommercial joy, and free, happy, wholesome recreation.

Take that as a guide-post, if you will; and then let me make my personal confession of a fisherman's faith.

I choose the recreation of angling for four reasons. First, because I like it: second, because it does no harm to anybody: third, because it brings me in touch with Nature, and with all sorts and conditions of men: fourth, because it helps me to keep fit for work and duty. Selah!

X

THE PATHLESS PROFESSION

It is a curious fact that there is no good guide-book to authorship. There are a few self-portraits, more or less convincing, of authors at work. There are many essays, more or less illuminating, upon the craft of writing in general, and upon the habits and procedure of certain great writers in particular. The best of these confessions and criticisms are excellent reading, full of entertainment and instruction for the alert and candid mind in every age and calling, and touched with a special, sympathetic interest for those young persons who have sternly resolved, or fondly dreamed, that they will follow a literary career. A volume of carefully selected material of this kind might be made attractive and rewarding to readers who are also intending authors. But the one thing for which such a book ought not to be taken, or mistaken, is a manual of the profession of literature.

The reasons for this appear to me quite as remarkable as the fact itself. The business of authors being to write, why should we not be able to gather from them such instruction in regard to writing, and the necessary preparation for it, as would make the pathway of authorship so plain that the wayfaring man though a fool need not err therein?

The answer to this question is an open secret, an instructive paradox.

There is no pathway of authorship.

It is a voyage, if you like; but there are no guide-posts in the sea. It is a flight, if you like; but there are no tracks in the air. It is certainly not a journey along a railway line, or a highroad, or even a well-marked trail.

In this it differs from other vocations like the Church, the Bar, the Army, the Navy, Engineering, Medicine, or Teaching. For each of these there is a pretty clearly defined path of preparatory study, with fixed gateways of examination along its course. When the last gate is passed and the young doctor is licensed to practice, the young clergyman ordained to preach, the young lawyer admitted to the bar, the path broadens into a road, which leads from one professional duty to another and brings him from task to task, if he is fortunate and industrious, with the regularity of a time-table, and, it must be added, with something of the monotony of a clock.

It is not so with the young intending author. There is no time of preparation prescribed, or even authoritatively advised, for him or for her. There are no fierce examiners standing like lions in the way. No hard-earned diploma, or certificate, or license is demanded. There are no set duties to be performed at certain times, like a case to be argued at the first session of the court in November, or an appendix to be removed next Thursday afternoon, or two sermons to be preached every Sunday. Intending authors, and for that matter practising authors, are like Milton's Adam and Eve when the closed gate of Paradise was behind them:

"*The world was all before them where to choose.*"

It looks very free and easy and attractive, this vocation of making books. All that the young writer has to do is to provide himself, or herself, with paper and a pen (or a typewriter), retire into a convenient room (almost any kind of a room will answer the purpose), and emerge with a book which a publisher will print, advertise, and sell, and which the public will read.

THE PATHLESS PROFESSION

And after that? Why, after that it looks freer and easier still. All that the successful writer has to do is to repeat the process with a new book at any convenient season.

But this very freedom, so alluring at a distance, becomes bewildering and troublesome at close range. The young intending author who has a serious ambition and a mind in thinking order very soon recognizes, either by the light of pure reason or by the glimmer of sad experience, that there are difficulties in this simple business of writing books which publishers will desire to print and the public to read. Many manuscripts are offered but few are chosen. How does one learn to cope with these difficulties and overcome them? How does one make ready to produce a manuscript which shall be reasonably sure of a place among the chosen few? By going to college, or by travel? By living in solitude, or in society? By imitating select models, or by cultivating a strenuous originality? By reading Plato, or *The Literary Digest?*

Nobody seems to know the right answer to these questions. Guesses are made at them. Universities announce courses in daily theme-writing. Schools of correspondence offer to teach the secrets of literature. Bureaus of Authorship are advertised. But the results produced by these various institutions are not consistent enough to be regarded as inevitable. Travel does not guarantee an observing mind, nor solitude a profound one; nor does society always refine the intelligence. The strenuous effort to be original often ends in a very common type of folly. Conscious imitation may be the sincerest flattery, but it rarely produces the closest resemblance.

Meantime, a sufficient number of authors, great and small, continue to arrive, as they always have arrived, from their native regions, by their own ways. Ask them how they got there, and they cannot tell you, even when they try to do so. The reason is because they do not know. There was no pathway. They travelled as they could. Power and skill came to them, sometimes suddenly, sometimes slowly, always inexplicably.

Do you suppose it is possible to explain how Shakespeare became able to write "Hamlet," or Milton to compose "Paradise Lost"? It is true that George Eliot describes "how she came to write fiction," and Stevenson gives an entertaining sketch of some of the methods in which he pursued his

THE PATHLESS PROFESSION

"own private end, which was to learn to write." But does George Eliot herself understand the secret of her preparation to create her vivid, revealing "Scenes from Clerical Life"? Or will the study of those favorite authors to whom Stevenson says he "played the sedulous ape," enable the young short-story-tellers really to reproduce his inimitable style?

In the middle of the nineteenth century several learned, industrious, and wise Americans were delivering lectures. Why did Emerson's crystallize into essays? Where did Hawthorne learn how to write "The Scarlet Letter,"—in Bowdoin College or in the Salem Custom-house? Could Thackeray have told you how he found the way from "The Luck of Barry Lyndon" to "Vanity Fair," or Dickens from "Sketches by Boz" to "Pickwick Papers"?

There is no other vocation of man into which "the unknown quantity" enters as largely as it does into authorship; and almost all writers who have won fame, even in a modest degree, if they are thoroughly candid, will confess to a not unpleasant experience of surprise at their own success.

Now all this implies an element of uncertainty

in the author's profession,—if, indeed, a vocation so pathless may be called a profession at all. In the regular and, so to speak, macadamized professions, those who follow the road with energy, fidelity, and fair intelligence may count upon a reasonable reward. But in the open field of literature it is impossible to foretell which one of a thousand aspirants will come to fame, or which ten will be able to earn a living.

It is for this reason, no doubt, that some instinct of prudence, or some pressure of necessity, has made many authors provide themselves with another bread-winner than the pen. When we consider how many well-known and even famous writers, from Chaucer to Conan Doyle, have had some avocation besides writing, we may justly conclude that there is hardly any human occupation, from diplomacy to doctoring, in which the intending author may not learn to write, and from which genius, or even talent, may not find a passage into literature. Charles Lamb's labor as a clerk in the East India House did not dim the luminous wit of his essays. William De Morgan's long life as a manufacturer of tiles did not prevent him, at last, from making his novels "somehow good." The career of James

THE PATHLESS PROFESSION

Ford Rhodes as an ironmaster was no bar to his notable success as a historian. Indeed, it almost seems as if some useful occupation, or at least some favorite recreation or pursuit, to bring the writer into unprofessional contact with the realities of life and the personalities of other men, may be more of a help than a hindrance to vital authorship.

Writing, in itself, is not an especially interesting or picturesque employment. Romance can make little of it. Even when the hero of a novel is a literary person, like Arthur Pendennis or David Copperfield, the things that interest us most happen to him outside of the book-room. It is what lies behind writing, and leads up to it, and flows into it, that really counts.

The biography of an author is almost interrupted when he takes his pen in hand.

Who would not ride with Scott on a summer raid through the Highlands, or walk with him and his dogs beside the Tweed, rather than watch him at work in the little room where he wrote "Waverley" by candle-light?

I think it was Byron who said something like this: "The moment in which a poem is conceived is one of infinite pleasure, the hours in which it is brought forth are full of the pains of labor." Of course I do not mean to deny that the author's vocation has its own inward delight and its own exceeding great reward. The delight lies in the conception of something that craves utterance: and the reward lies in the production of something that goes out alive into the world. A true call to the vocation of literature is both inward and outward: a strong desire of self-expression, and a proved power of communicating thought and feeling through the written word.

The wish to write merely for the sake of being a writer, if I may so describe a vague ambition which vexes many young persons, is rather a small and futile thing, and seldom leads to happiness, usefulness, or greatness.

Literature has been made by men and women who became writers because they had something to say and took the necessary pains to learn how to say it.

But how did this happen to these men and women? What brought them to this happy pass where the inward call to self-expression was confirmed by the outward power to interest readers? Who can tell?

THE PATHLESS PROFESSION

It looks simple. And no doubt there is a certain element of simplicity in the necessary processes of learning to spell, to construct sentences, to use words correctly, to develop plots, to recognize rhymes, and to observe metres. But there is a mystery in it, after all.

From Shakespeare's deepest tragedy to Kipling's most rattling ditty, from Wordsworth's loftiest ode to Dobson's lightest lyric, from Victor Hugo's biggest romance to De Maupassant's briefest tale, from Plato's profoundest dialogue to Chesterton's most paradoxical monologue, from George Eliot's "Romola" to Miss Alcott's "Little Women," every bit of literature, great or small, has a measure of magic in it, and ultimately is no more explicable than life itself.

XI

A MID-PACIFIC PAGEANT

WE live in a period of historic pageants. The world, fatigued by the monotony of manners and dress which civilization is imposing on its once gaily variegated folks, seeks a brief escape from the tiresome prospect of a standardized humanity. It loves to recall for an hour the fanciful costumes and scenes, the dramatic and symbolic actions of the past. History lays aside her dusty dignity and goes into moving pictures.

London and Paris revisualize their barbaric childhood and see themselves in the fierce conflicts and gallant enterprises of youth. Alfred repels the Danes, Charlemagne assembles his chivalry, William of Normandy conquers Britain, Columbus discovers America, Henry Hudson sails the *Half Moon* up Manhattan Bay, the Pilgrim Fathers set their possessive foot on the stern and rock-bound coast of Massachusetts, the French monks penetrate the Middle West by the broad avenue of the Missis-

A MID-PACIFIC PAGEANT

sippi, and the Spanish friars build their missions in California.

The "first settlers" of North Hingham, and New Utrecht, and West Colbyville, and Calvinton, and Sauk City Centre, and Almadena, and many another place dear to its inhabitants, revisit the frail glimpses of glory and show their ancient garb and authority before their proud descendants.

The local audience gleefully recognizes the familiar performers in their unfamiliar guise. Old Bill Hodson as Columbus awakens applause which he never received as postmaster. Hi Waite, the plumber, makes an immense success as William Penn. Maude Alice Magillicuddy is ravishing as the Indian Princess with beaded leggings. The Reverend Adoniram Jump is welcomed with hilarity as Bloodeye Ben the stern and deadly Sheriff. Multitudinous laughter, and cheering, and hearty handclapping run around the encircling throng. But behind the noise there is an eager attention, a serious pleasure, a sense of imaginative satisfaction. The village, the town, even the conventional city, has been linked up for an hour with the wonderful past, in which strange things happened and the raiment of life was a Joseph's coat of many colors.

CAMP-FIRES

Were events really so much more significant and entertaining in old times than they are now? Or is it only an illusion of perspective, an illustration of the law that

> "the past must win
> A glory by its being far,
> And orb into the perfect star
> We saw not when we moved therein"?

Will the people of 2000 A. D. look back to the era when the airplane and wireless telegraphy were discovered as the true and only age of romance? Who knows? What difference? For us, in these complicated days, it is a delight to reverse our vision and see things pass before us in large outline, simpler and more striking,—perhaps truer, perhaps only easier to think we understand.

One of the most vivid and delightful pageants that I have ever seen was in April of 1920, on an island in the middle of the Pacific Ocean, at the hundredth anniversary of Christian Missions in Hawaii. It was memorable not for its costly splendor and famous audience, but for the clearness and significance of its scenes and the wondrous beauty of the stage on which it was set. Moreover, along with the

A MID-PACIFIC PAGEANT

pageant and around it, before and after, there ran an accompaniment which illuminated and emphasized its meaning and added infinitely to its charm. Of this I will speak first.

The Hawaiian Islands are the *carrefour* of the watery highways between East and West. Lay a course from Tokyo to Panama, from Vancouver to Melbourne, from Seattle to Singapore, from San Francisco to Manila, from Los Angeles to Hongkong, and your lines will make a star in the sea not far from Honolulu.

Two thousand miles away is the mainland of North America,—four or five thousand, the mainland of Asia,—far to southward, the sprinkled isles of Polynesia,—far to northward the rocky, frosty chain of the Aleutians. The vast sapphire solitude of the Pacific encircles the Territory of Hawaii with a beautiful isolation which the adventurous spirit of man has transformed into an opening for worldwide commerce. The lonely place has become a port of call for all nations.

You must not think of these islands as a cluster of coral reefs, embowered in palms and sweltering under the rays of a tropical sun. They are a group of five, each one large enough to make a little state in New England or Europe, and separated by wide stretches of seldom-quiet sea.

From Oahu, the only island I visited, you can just see Molokai with the lofty peak of Maui behind it, like a lonely purple cloud on the horizon. Away to the southeast the big bulk of Hawaii, where the volcanoes are still on active duty, is lost in distance. Away to the northwest the sharp peaks and cloven valleys of Kauai are invisible.

But Oahu contains in itself the makings of a tiny complete continent. There are two ranges of real mountains, which rose from the bottom of the sea some twenty thousand years ago, "by drastic lift of pent volcanic fires." Wind and weather have carved them into jagged ridges and pinnacles four thousand feet high. Between them lies the broad upland plain of Waialua and Ewa. The mountainsides are furrowed by deep glens and ravines, sharpest on the northeast side where the rains are heaviest, gentler on the south and west where the vales spread out, fanlike, into the broad sugar-plantations of the coast, and the virid fields of springing rice.

The foliage of the hills and valleys is wonderfully varied. The pale green of the *kukui* contrasts

A MID-PACIFIC PAGEANT

vividly with the dark green of the *koa* and the *ohia*. Long avenues of sombre ironwood-trees with drooping threadlike leaves stretch beside the road. The huge banyans and monkey-pods spread their tabernacles of pillared shade. The *hau* twists and twines its smooth trunks and branches into wide arbors, as if it were half tree and half vine. Stiff little *papayas*, with round, flat tops like parasols, lift their clusters of delicious fruit as high as they can reach. Plumy mangoes conceal rich treasure among their pendent foliage. Breadfruits expand their broad palmated leaves. The bright feathery green of the algaroba-trees (springing from a few seed-pods which a priest brought from the mainland in his pocket not many years ago) has flowed far and wide over the lowlands and slopes, making open groves where the cattle feed on the fallen beans, and tangled thickets full of needle-sharp thorns.

For purely tropical effect there are the bananas, with broad bending leaves, always flourishing and generally dishevelled; and the palms, a score of different kinds,—the smooth columnar royal palm with green-gray trunk and bushy head high-lifted; the slender cocoa-palm with corrugated bole, often slanting or curving, and heavy fruit half concealed by its tousled fronds; the rough-bodied palmetto; and many another little palm of the kind that withers and pines in the hallways of our Northern houses, but here spreads its hands abroad and wrestles gaily with the wind.

The wind,—the wind, the glorious life-giving trade-wind is the good angel of the Hawaiian Islands. It is the only big wind that I ever loved.

Nine months of the year it blows out of the northeast over the lapis-lazuli plain of the Pacific, bringing health and joy on its wings. The great white clouds come with it, like treasure-fleets with high-piled sails. Above the mountains they pause, tangled and broken among the peaks. They change to dark gray and blue and almost black. They let down their far-brought riches, now in showers as soft as melted sunshine, now in torrential *douches* of seeming-solid rain. But the big trade-wind still blows, drawing down the valleys, tossing the palm-fronds, waving the long boughs of the algarobas and the slender tops of the ironwoods, refreshing the city streets and the sun-warmed beaches, where perhaps not a drop of rain has fallen, rustling through the fragrant gardens, and passing out to

A MID-PACIFIC PAGEANT

sea with a merry train of whitecaps. There you shall see him reassembling his snowy squadrons and flotillas of the air, driving them southward to refresh other thirsty islands.

It is the trade-wind that accounts for the livable and lovable climate of Hawaii, in which a native race of extraordinary beauty and strength developed, and people of America and Europe and Asia can make their homes without loss of health or working vigor. The thermometer, elsewhere a recorder of weather-torments, here loses its terrors, for it moves between 60° for winter's cold and 85° for summer's heat. Even when the sun is most ardent there is always a breeze in the shade that will cool you gently without a chill.

Honolulu is no siesta-city, where the shops are closed at noonday and the merchants retire to hammocks. It is a busy, thriving, modern town, which works full time every week-day, and where the telephone rings without ceasing. Its suburbs are reaching out Ewa way, Waikiki way, Nuuanu and Manoa way, threading house after house on the trolley-lines. It has a good water-supply and a clean harbor front. Best of all, its civic life has a core of intelligence and public spirit, embodied in men and women of missionary stock, who feel that they are citizens of no mean city, and are resolved to have it look well and be well.

Yet it is astonishing how unobtrusive the city is, how little it mars the landscape. I often found myself forgetting that it was there. Our friendly hosts lived in a house with broad *lanai* and long *pergola*, on the shoulder of one of the lower hills sloping down from Mt. Tantalus. Look out between the royal palms on the terrace, and you will see the city almost submerged in a sea of greenery, like a swimmer floating on his back in tranquil waters. Beyond the long beach is a lagoon of translucent *aqua marina*, and beyond that the silver curve of the surf on the coral reef, and beyond that the intense cobalt blue of the Pacific. To the left lies the fulvous shape of Diamond Head, like a lion *couchant*, looking out to sea. Farther to the east, and sweeping around into the north, rise the dark peaks of the Koolau Range, embracing the Manoa Valley. Here and there you see the roofs of houses among the trees, the long arcades of Punahou School, the white façade of the College of Hawaii, the many windows of the Mid-Pacific Institute,—(never a place with so many fine schools as Honolulu!). But

A house with broad *lanai* and long *pergola*.

A MID-PACIFIC PAGEANT

for the most part it is a tree-top view, like that from the cottage in the last scene of "Peter Pan."

Under the trees, and clambering over them, what flowers and vines! Tall hedges of hibiscus all abloom with scarlet and white and rose and yellow of every shade: masses of climbing Bougainvillea covered with light purple or flame-colored flowers: fragrant plumarias with clusters of pale white, or ivory yellow, or shell pink: lilies, milk-white or tawny orange: allamanda vines thickly set with rich golden trumpets, and honeysuckles with coral red: oleanders, white and rose: acacias, drooping aureate plumes, or clustering pink blossoms like apple-trees in May: intense burning red of Poinsettia; heavenly blue of a tree whose name I do not know, but whose rare beauty I shall never forget. They tell me that later in the season the long wall around Oahu College, where the night-blooming cereus covers the stones, will break into a glory of white bloom. But I can't wait for that.

The sea is as rich in colors as the land. The water changes its hues like peacock-feathers. The fish beneath it are vivid as if they had been dipped in rainbows. You may see them in glass tanks at the Aquarium,—weird, amazing creatures, some with

CAMP-FIRES

long bills like birds, others with floating plumes and pennants,—streaked and striped and speckled, as if a mad painter had decorated them. I could not get rid of the feeling that they had been fabricated for the amusement of the visitor.

But when I went on a picnic in the lonely, lovely bay of Hanama I saw them and caught them among the coral and lava rocks, at the foot of huge cliffs where the long waves rolled and broke in fountains of high-spouting foam. Those fish were quite as quaint as their cousins in the Aquarium: pale green, fringed with azure and banded obliquely with broad strips of black; bright blue, with orange fins, and on the sides a damascened pattern of mauve and apple-green; dark green, bordered with dark blue, and inlaid across the body with lozenges of crimson.

I tell you we caught fish there that were absolutely incredible. I disbelieved in them even while they flapped upon the rocks. But one I firmly believed in,—the golden giant, with a beak like an eagle's and a tail like a lyre-bird's, which the lady avowed she saw swimming disdainfully around her hook in the clear water. She angled for him with the patience of a saint, the hope of a poet, and the

A MID-PACIFIC PAGEANT

courage of a hero. The waves swirled about her knees; the spray dashed over her shoulders; her mind was firmly set upon that preposterous, scornful fish. But she never caught him. That is why I believe in him.

On the way home from our motor-rides we would stop at some convenient place,—oftenest at the long beach of Kahala,—and have a swim in the sea. The water was warm, and soft as silk. Within the lagoon it was still, but on the reef beyond the big waves were roaring, (as Bottom says,) "gently as any sucking dove." Bathing in the Pacific is a pastime fit for Paradise. I trust that some equivalent substitute for it will be provided in that world where, St. John tells us, "There shall be no more sea."

At Waikiki Beach we tried the surf-riding in a long, narrow, outrigger-canoe. You paddle out a quarter of a mile, beyond the breakers; then you wait for a big roller,—a *decuman*, the Romans called it, believing that the tenth wave was always the largest. But the muscular Hawaiian boy who steers, (adequately clothed in a loin-cloth and his bronzed skin,) knows nothing of Latin superstitions. He feels by instinct when the roller is coming; swings the dugout toward the beach and gives a yell; everybody paddles hard; the water swells beneath us, rises, sweeps forward, breaks into foam; and the canoe is carried swiftly on the crest, smothered in spray,—impelled by an immeasurable force, yet guided straight by human will and skill, unable to turn back, yet safe in darting forward,—till the wave sinks in soft ripples on the sand.

That is the joy of motion: to ride on something that is infinitely stronger than you, and yet to be the master of your course. It is the thrill of tobogganing, skate-sailing, air-planing, surf-riding,—to feel yourself borne along by the irresistible, but still the captain of your own little ship!

I have delayed too long, perhaps, in the description of the scene and the accompaniments of the Mid-Pacific Pageant of which I set out to tell you. Yet here (and often elsewhere in the world,) the stage belongs to the play, and the *décor* is part of the action.

In the spacious park of Punahou School, (founded by the missionaries,) there is a broad playground called Alexander Field, (given by the descendants of missionaries,) and behind this rises Rocky Hill,

A MID-PACIFIC PAGEANT

a considerable height, with grassy slopes strewn with blocks of lava, and a shallow valley in the centre, leading by easy gradations toward the summit.

The usual arrangement of an outdoor play is reversed. The audience and the chorus occupy the level: the actors move in the amphitheatre above them, going and coming by their palm-screened exits,—*makai*, seaward,—*mauka*, toward the mountains.

Seven hundred voices are in the chorus, gathered from various schools and colleges, including Hawaiians, Filipinos, Japanese, Chinese, Portuguese, Porto Ricans, and Anglo-Saxons. In the audience there seem to be ten or twelve thousand, scattered over the playing-field and the grassy slopes and terraces around it. The pageant represents the history of Hawaii for a hundred years, from the arrival of the first missionaries from New England in 1820, down to the present day.

It is difficult to compress so long a period into so short a show. To tell the truth, there are some ancient ways and manners in the record which must be left invisible; and some modern episodes which the most raging realist would not care to put upon the stage; and some political complications and intrigues which not even the most confidential chorus and the most elaborate tableaux could fully present. But the main story, the story of the things that really count and signify, is simple enough. Miss Ethel Damon has told it with admirable skill in her scenario and text; and Miss Jane Winne has preluded and accompanied it with excellent music.

The performance opens with Beethoven's "Hymn of Creation," rendered by the Hawaiian Band. Then comes a choral overture suggesting the ancient state of civil war on the islands, the unrest and confusion caused by the old *tabu* system, and the comparative unity and peace brought by the victories of that beneficent tyrant, Kaméhaméha I, the Charlemagne of savages. Then comes the appeal to the imagination through the eyes, in color, movement, and human action.

You must know a little about the history in order to follow the story closely, and to supply in imagination the darker elements of human sacrifice and infanticide and drunkenness and debauchery which so nearly turned the Hawaiian drama into an irremediable tragedy.

But even without this knowledge you can feel

A MID-PACIFIC PAGEANT

the magic of the scene; the glorious setting of the play between the mountains and the sea; the little human shapes coming and going along the grassy trails, among the scattered rocks and wind-tossed trees; bare, brown arms and legs glistening in the sun, many-colored garments fluttering in the breeze, files and groups and crowds of men and women and children forming and dissolving around certain dominant figures,—a chapter of the human romance, unfolded on the breast of nature, beneath the open sky, in the light of the Eternal Presence.

The first picture shows the royal state of Kaméhaméha the Great, the native conqueror of the islands. Ancient rites and customs are displayed: old women beating bark for *tapa*-cloth, old men preparing *poi*, chiefs and chiefesses paying homage, commoners bringing their tribute of food and garments, all prostrating themselves before the monarch; a procession of soldiers and priests, carrying tall standards of war and hideous idols, the ugliest and most sacred of which is the red god of battle; a great feast spread on the ground; *hula-hula* dancing by beautiful damsels with mild reservations. It is a confused, barbaric scene, dominated by the tall old King in his cloak and helmet of red and yellow feathers. He is gloomy and unsatisfied, all-powerful and sad: his red god gives him no counsel for the using of his power. He vainly seeks enlightenment from his oldest priest and from one of the white men in his train. Silent and sombre, "the Lonely One" stalks off toward the sea, and the crowd melts away.

The second picture shows the breaking of the ancient *tabu* system and the destruction of the idols. The new King, Liholiho, is afraid at first, but his reluctance is overcome by the Queen, and the Queen Regent, who is in effect the most powerful person in the islands. It is the women who have suffered most from the tyranny of *tabu*, which forbade them to eat with their fathers, husbands, or male children, and prohibited them from using the most nourishing foods, under penalty of death. Womanhood rebels. The Queen eats a forbidden banana with her little son. Thus the *tabu* is badly cracked if not smashed. The Queen Regent argues, (and perhaps threatens,) with the King until he yields. The idols are thrown down, trampled under foot, burned. The bands of ancient, cruel superstition are loosed.

(But note here, reader, a strange fact unknown

A MID-PACIFIC PAGEANT

to the audience. The native Hawaiian actors cast for the part of iconoclasts, alarmed by the mysterious death of one of their number a few days before, declined to play the rôle of idol-breakers. Their place has to be supplied by Filipino and Chinese actors, whose subconscious minds have no roots of association with these particular images. Even in the twentieth century, as the Romans said long ago, "you can't expel nature with a pitchfork,"—nor with a pageant.)

The third and fourth pictures show the arrival of the Christian missionaries from New England,—seven men and seven women, with five children,—and the beginning of their work. The crisis of peril in their first reception, the gentle persuasions by which they win a welcome and permission to stay, the busyness of their early days in teaching the gentle savages the rudiments of learning and the arts of peace, are well depicted. The contrast in dress between the styles of New Haven and of Hawaii in 1820 is striking. The compromise invented for the native women in the shapeless form of the *holoku*, (a kind of outdoor nightgown,) is not altogether successful, but brilliant colors save it. Conch-shells call the children to open-air schools.

CAMP-FIRES

Spinning-wheels are brought out. Needles get busy. A great white cross is disclosed at the top of the hill. Allegorical figures of Faith, Hope, and Charity, clad respectively in blue, pale green, and rose *chiffon*, flutter around, pretty and futile as allegorical figures usually are. The new era has begun. The details of hard work and struggle and danger and privation are written in the diaries and letters and records of the missionaries. Only the symbolic picture is shown here,—Christian love and courage setting out to rescue a generous, warm-hearted race from the degrading vices of so-called civilization without a religion, and to heal the poison-sores left by the fetters of hoary superstition.

The most dramatic episode in the story is shown in the fifth picture. Kapiolani, a noble princess of the islands, resolves to defy the goddess *Pele*, fierce mistress of undying fire, who dwells in the seething, flame-spouting crater of Kilauea. The princess, personated by a stately Hawaiian woman, climbs the crag on which a mimic volcano has been built. The volcano emits sufficient red fire and black smoke to suggest the terrifying reality to the imagination. The princess picks the sacred berries, which it is death to touch on the way up the moun-

A MID-PACIFIC PAGEANT

tain, stands on the brink of the crater and eats them, scornfully tossing the stones into the lake of fire and crying "Jehovah is my God!" The great defiance is accomplished and the power of *Pele* over the souls of men is broken. Tennyson wrote one of his latest poems, *Kapiolani*, on this theme.

(But remember, reader, what happened only a few years ago in the wonderful Bishop Museum, where the antiquities of the island are collected. A miniature *heiau*,—temple of the old gods,—was set up in the central hall. It was almost completed; council-chamber of the priests, enclosure walled with blocks of lava, black altar overshadowed by grinning idols,—all done but the slab for human sacrifice. A Hawaiian youth, working upon the roof, stepped by accident on the glass skylight of the hall, and fell through. His head was shattered on the altar, his blood stained the sands around it. Crowds of the Hawaiians came to look at the place. They shook their heads gravely and whispered one to another: "That was the only way,—no human sacrifice, no temple!")

Come back to the pageant on the sunny hillside. The four remaining pictures display the reign of law under the Magna Charta of King Kaméhaméha

CAMP-FIRES

III; the development of modern industries; the union of Hawaii with America in 1898, and a review of the progress of a century. There is considerable allegory in the presentation; but the redeeming touch of reality is ever present in the fact that the chief actors are the descendants of the missionaries and of the Hawaiians whom they came so far to teach.

In the last scene more than two thousand people, from all the Christian Schools and the so-called "constructive agencies" of all races on the islands, take part. With waving flags and many-colored banners they stream up the green hill. Forming a huge open triangle, with the point toward the great cross at the top, the living symbol hangs poised in the light of the descending sun. The palms wave and rustle in the breeze. The white surf murmurs on the distant reef. The blue Pacific heaves and sparkles far away. The light clouds drift across the turquoise sky. Over the fair stage and the finished pageant sounds Haydn's glorious hymn, "The Heavens Are Telling the Glory of God."

Shall I leave my story of pictures, impressions, memories, and hopes in Hawaii, just there? What can I add to it that may not darken counsel by words without knowledge?

A MID-PACIFIC PAGEANT

The beautiful territory in the sea is full of people now, gathered from many lands, speaking diverse tongues, and thinking different thoughts,—Hawaiians, and half-Hawaiians, Caucasians, Filipinos, Koreans, Chinese, and one hundred and twenty thousand Japanese,—as many from Japan as from any four of the other races. Problems of race-mixture, of education, of capital and labor, of civic progress or reaction, of democratic government without class tyranny, must be met and solved.

The people of Hawaii have their work cut out for them. The Government of the United States must stand by them steadily. There will be showers, storms, tempests of unrest; but I think there will be no cataclysm of destruction. The spirit which guided the missionaries will prove equal to its new tasks. And in due time there will be a new star, a bright tranquil all-Pacific star, in the flag of the United States of America.

XII

JAPONICA

THE plan was to take Paula to Japan, in fulfilment of a promise I made her when she was a little tiny daughter; to have a brief, glorious vacation there, with some collateral trout-fishing; and then to come home and write a luminous, comprehensive, conclusive monograph on the Japanese Problem.

This well-laid plan went "a-gley." The first part of the programme rolled off splendidly. But now I come to the second part and find it can't be done. I know too much and too little.

Japan is no longer a mere name to me: it is a real country, a wonderful land, a great nation. Its very simplicity makes it hard to comprehend and explain. The Far Eastern Question is too large to be solved by an anthropological dogma, or settled by a snappy phrase.

"The Yellow Peril" is an invention worthy of the yellow press. The writers who deal with this nightmare kind of stuff, like Houston Chamberlain and Karl Pearson and the rest, are intellectual neurotics, very jumpy and with a subconscious homicidal tendency. You would not trust them to run a mowing-machine or a trading-schooner.

Rudyard Kipling was right in saying,

"Oh, East is East, and West is West".

but was he right (except by metrics), in adding,

"And never the twain shall meet"?

In fact they have met already. The temporal reduction of the spatial globe, the commercial ambition of the West, the overflow of the crowded populations of the East, have already brought them together on a long line of contacts. The question now is how shall they live and work together so as to promote the welfare and true happiness of the world.

This is not a question to be decided offhand, even by the youngest and most cocksure of anthropologists. It must be worked out slowly, with patient good-will, and careful application of old, general, well-tried principles of reason and justice. *Solvitur ambulando*.

So I have joyfully jettisoned the idea of that convincing monograph on the Japanese Problem. Sitting here at the wide window of my little bungalow on the Maine coast, looking out over fir-clad islands, blue sea, and mountain-shores (which remind me vividly of Japan), I shall only try to sketch a few memories of our journey in that delectable island. The title of the rambling paper is *Japonica*, which means, "things of or pertaining to Japan."

TOKYO IN THE RAIN

Coming into Yokohama in one of the fine Toyo Kisen ships, on a gray dripping day, we saw little to interest us, except the home-coming joy of our Japanese fellow passengers, children and all. We wondered why they should love such a wet, drab country.

Tokyo did not enlighten us. It is big without grandeur: a wide-spread, flat, confused city, with interesting and even picturesque spots in it, art treasures hidden in museums and private houses, some fifteen hundred Buddhist temples and Shinto shrines (a few of which are noteworthy,) a hundred and twenty-five Christian churches, and many gardens lovely even in the rain.

The warm hospitality of the accomplished American Ambassador, the Japanese Foreign Minister, the cordial missionaries of the great Methodist schools at Aoyama Gakuin, Doctor and Mrs. Corell of the Episcopal Church, and many other friends old and new; the comfort of the Imperial Hotel and the intelligent and informing conversation of its manager Mr. Hayashi, whom I had known years ago as a student in New York; the amusement of expeditions through the crowded, many-colored street called the Ginza; the pathetic interest of a visit to the huge shabby-splendid temple of Asakusa Kwannon, most popular of city fanes—these were consolations and entertainments for which we were grateful.

But they did not quite lift us out of the depression of a rainy week in Tokyo. The air was dead, streets mud, cherry-blossoms fallen. So we determined to cut loose from the capital and go up to Nikko, weather permitting or not.

RED TEMPLES AND TALL TREES

Five hours on a comfortable railway carried us northward through a coastal plain of small square fields of rice and wheat, barley and millet, rape, radishes, onions, and taro, all carefully brought up by hand; then eastward, through a country of rising foot-hills with horizontal villages and farmhouses tucked away among the trees and every inch of valley-bottom cultivated to the limit; and so at last, through copses of cherry and maple and pine, splashed with rose-pink of wild azaleas, to the famous avenue of tall *Cryptomeria Japonica* leading up to the scarlet shrines of Nikko.

It is a small mountain town, whose name means "sunny splendor," but whose glory is nested in coverts of evergreen shade.

The red-lacquered bridge that springs with a delicate, effortless curve across the rushing Daiyagawa at the upper end of the village, is too sacred for common use. Only Imperial Envoys and High Priests and Holy Pilgrimages twice a year may tread it. But they say that bold village boys on dark nights climb the secluding gates and scamper swiftly over the forbidden arch.

The temples are all on the north side of the stream; terraced on the steep hillside that rises toward the snow-capped range of Nantai-san: embowered in a sacred grove more majestic than Dodona. The stately *sugi*, sisters to the giant sequoia of California, are the pillars of the green roof. Russet-trunked *hinoki*, with cypress-like foliage, and plumy *retinosporas*, are scattered through the forest. In the more open spaces are budding maples and birches. In the courtyards double-cherries are in radiant bloom. Far and wide the ground is spread with soft moss and feathery ferns. Amid all this natural splendor, so tranquil and so rich, the temples stand on their gray stone terraces, adorned with opulence of art and man's device.

The prevailing color is a deep Indian red. But there is not a hue of the rainbow that is not lavished somewhere on carved rafter or columned gateway, pierced screen or panelled ceiling, treasure-house, baldachin, drum-tower or bell-tower. The spirit of the grotesque runs riot in the portrayal of unknown animals and supernatural beings. But realism has its turn in graphic portraits of familiar birds and beasts, like Sakai's twelve hawks, and the "sleeping cat" of Hidari Jingoro, which makes you drowsy to look at it.

Nothing "towers" at Nikko, except the trees and the one stately vermeil pagoda. The temples are more broad than lofty. Their green-bronze roofs, curving gently outward, project in wide eaves. Their doors and beams and ridge-poles are adorned with bosses, rosettes, and hinges of gold or gleaming black metal. They have the effect of immense jewel-boxes, covered with decoration and crammed with treasures.

God made the forest. Then man said, "Let us see what I can do." So he made the shrines.

They are in effect the mausolea of two famous Japanese warriors and rulers.

The eastern and more elaborate group is dedicated to Ieyasu, the first Shogun of the Tokugawa clan, a great general, mighty hunter, and patron of the fine arts. He pacified Japan by killing his enemies in 1600, and began that long régime of seclusion and comparative tranquillity which lasted until the downfall of the Shogunate in 1867.

The western group belongs to Iemitsu, his grandson, and is considered less important. To us it seemed no less attractive, perhaps because we went there on a sunshiny day, when the double-cherries were in glory around the old Futa-ara shrine, and the clear mountain rivulets were sparkling through the temple compound and overflowing the granite water-basins in thin sheets like liquid glass.

Three days we spent in roaming up and down these terraces, through rain and shine; and all the time thousands of Japanese men, women, and children, pilgrims or excursionists, were coming and going, gazing and wondering, listening devoutly to the discourse of their guides.

The holy of holies of the Ieyasu temples was opened to us by special permit from the Abbot. It was so rich that I can't remember much of it.

But I remember that outside the Honden was a little pavilion tenanted by an old-maidenish priestess, very small and dainty in crimson kirtle and snowy cap and surplice. At the request of visitors she would rise from her meditative seat on the floor and perform a quaint, decorous, graceful dance "to drive away the evil spirits." She was of an inscrutable age; but a youthful soul smiled through the lattice of her gravity; her steps and motions were sure and supple. She carried a fan in one hand and a softly, silvery tinkling instrument in the other. These she waved toward us thrice at certain turns in the performance. It was fascinating.

We came back when no one was looking and persuaded her by silver inducements to do it again and again. Each time her smile was a little brighter. "I don't feel any evil spirits coming or going," said Paula, "but I simply *must* get the steps of that dance."

CAMP-FIRES

HIGHLAND WATERS

All around Nikko there are fine waterfalls,—a score of them within easy walking distance. In the mountains beyond there are many lakes, two of which have a certain renown. Chusenji, the larger, nearly 4,500 feet above the sea, is a modest summer resort. Yumoto, more than 5,000 feet up, is smaller and hardly frequented at all except for the hot sulphur baths at the head of the lake. To these highland waters we resolved to go.

The motor road for some three miles followed the broad stony bed of the Daiya-gawa. There had been a spate a few days before, which carried away the smaller bridges. Gangs of coolies were deftly rebuilding them with bamboo as we passed. Presently the valley narrowed, the road gave out, and we began to foot it on the 'rickshaw path. Steep cliffs overshadowed us. Cascades on tributary streams trailed their white scarves from shoulders of the hills. The path zigzagged up the mountainside. Three or four rustic tea-houses, perched at convenient distances, commanded gorgeous views down the valley. The main river roared far below.

But the memorable beauty of that breath-taking

JAPONICA

climb was the flood of wild azaleas streaming down every hillside through the lace-leafy woods of early spring. From pale rose to deep flame, from rich mauve to faintest pink, their color shaded and shimmered, now massed along a level ridge, now pouring down a rocky slope—a glory no more wonderful, but more delicate and entrancing than the giant rhododendrons blooming along a Pennsylvania brook, or the high laurels beside a little river of South Jersey.

Useless plants, all of them, except to the soul of man!

Finally topping the crest, we came through a level wood of birch and maple, to the head of the famous Kegon Cataract where the Daiya-gawa rushes from the lake through a ten-foot rift in the rock, and plunges straight down two hundred and fifty feet into the churning pool below. The clouds of spray, the ceaseless thunder, the dizzying change of the fall from swift motion to seeming immobility, were bewildering and benumbing. Hundreds of hapless Japanese lovers, bent on suicide, have thought this a fitting place to leap out of life into Nirvana.

Chusenji is a lovely lake. High hills embrace it. Nantai-san soars above it. Bird-peopled woods en-

CAMP-FIRES

circle it, except at the outlet, where there is a small village with half a dozen big Japanese inns on one bank of the stream and the Lakeside Hotel on the other. It is a comfortable hostelry—Japanese exterior, European furnishing. We were the only staying guests, and well cared for by the landlord and his whole family—including two little Breathless Boys, who did everything on the full run, and made up for their blunders by smiling good-will.

Yumoto is a very different lake, more Alpine, more surprising. It lies on the knees of the mountain-gods, like a beautiful fairy child. Primeval pine-trees form a dense grove round the lower part of the lake; steaming sulphur springs issue from the bare slopes at the upper end. At the very foot there is a tiny islet, dividing the clear green water, which drops straightaway over the cliff in a broad, wrinkled, rippling curtain, like white watered-silk, two hundred feet long.

In the green dell below, perhaps a hundred yards from the fall, a fine pool has formed, with a large foam-covered backwater on the opposite side of the stream. Arriving there at twilight one evening in mid-May, after a seven-mile tramp, Paula and I could not bear to push on without trying our luck.

The three-ounce rod sent the tiny "Queen of the Water" and "Royal Coachman" fifty feet across the stream, to the edge of the foam. The white sheet was broken by the tail of a fish. A quick strike hooked him. He rushed gamely down the rapids, played hard for a good quarter of an hour, and then came to the net,—a plump, American brook-trout of a pound and a quarter weight. Thrice the performance was repeated before the night fell. Then we climbed the steep ascent, and trudged over snow-drifts in the dark pine-wood, and through the sulphur-scented moorland, to the little Nanma Inn, where we found a warm Japanese welcome and had the whole doll-house at our disposal.

Three days we fished that stream between Yumoto and Chusenji, winding along the edge of a wild Alpine plain covered with reeds and bamboo-grass. The fish were plentiful,—rainbows, and *fontinalis*, and pink-finned native trout; but the water was too high and drumlie for fly-fishing. My average was fifteen fish a day.

Our guide was a cheerful Japanese boatman named Ochiai, or something like that. He knew ten or twelve words of English, and was a passionate bait-fisher and a thorough gentleman. I remember the night when we arrived at the hamlet of Shobu-no-hama in a pelting storm. He introduced us to the humble cottage of a friend, where we sheltered beside the family-fire of charcoal while the boat was being prepared to take us down the lake. Hot tea was served, as a matter of course. When we scrambled down to the skiff, Ochiai brought up a dripping, apologetic peddler with a huge pack, and explained politely, — "Zis gent'man wet, — Chusenji?" We took him in, and the boatman sculled slowly down to the foot of the lake, while Paula-san and I sang college songs to keep ourselves warm.

THE HEART'S CAPITAL OF JAPAN

Kyoto, with its 450,000 inhabitants, lies in the fertile Yamashiro plain, ringed by green and lofty hills. For many centuries it was the seat of the Imperial Court, until Tokyo displaced it in 1868. But it still remains, I think, the chief city in the heart of Japan.

Here the ancient arts and ways are more purely preserved; here the old traditions centre; here a visitor does not have to witness, as Lafcadio Hearn said in his last days of Tokyo, "the sorry sight of one civilization trampling the life out of another."

Mind you, I don't say that what is taking place in Tokyo and other great seaport towns is wrong or evitable. I only say that if you want the flavor and the tone of the original Japan, you must see Kyoto, and smaller cities of that type, and, above all, the countryside.

We spent a fortnight in and around Kyoto, with headquarters at the Miyako Hotel, where the conversation of the manager, Mr. Hamaguchi, was delightful and illuminating. He told us the meaning of many things in Japanese life and philosophy, and best of all he advised us what to skip in our sightseeing.

All kinds of pictures from that fortnight are stored in memory's "go-down." I can take out one after another and hang it on the wall, as a Japanese would do with his *kakemonos*.

There is the famous Cherry Blossom Dance, in the biggest tea-house on the Kamo-gawa, where forty *geishas* weave intricate, slow designs of color and movement on the stage, while a double-dozen of women musicians twang *samisens*, slap drums, and chant weird nasal songs. There is the stately Noh Drama, performed on the century-old stage of the Nishi Hongwanji temple, by actors who have inherited their calling and traditions through generations,—gorgeous costumes, symbolic action, classic dialogue, mostly tragic themes, with some consecrated comic episodes, the chorus intoning a running commentary, the absorbed audience following the play with their books,—it is a highly intellectual and at the same time eye-appealing performance, something like the revival of a Greek play at Oxford or Harvard, yet different as the East differs from the West. There are visits to a few well-chosen temples. The golden splendor of the great Chion-in. The tranquil charm of Kurodani on its shady hill, with its long inner corridors where the "nightingale floors" twitter beneath your stockinged feet, its rooms adorned with rare paintings and silken broideries, and its secluded garden where the iris is in bloom around the pond. The delicate beauty of the Golden Pavilion and the Silver Pavilion in their landscape setting; and one little temple among the trees, whose name I never knew, but which Paula said she loved "because it seemed so lonely, and nobody told us to go there."

Certain scenes and incidents are vivid in my mind. Visits to workshops, where deft Japanese fingers are busy with delicate work of tapestry,

The temple-garden where the iris blooms around the pond.

damascene, lacquer, and carving. Preaching in the little Union Church, and lecturing to a thousand eager students at Doshisha University. Luncheon with Miss Denton of the Girls' School, that wonderful American lady who knows Kyoto better than the Japanese and whom they all love. "Ceremonial tea" at Doctor Saiki's house, where the gentle daughter of Nippon who performs the gracious ritual is the mother of nine and looks no older than one of her own children.

Of all Kyoto days none was brighter than that on which we walked with the Shivelys over the sacred mountain of Hiei-san. The long trail up through the steep, stately forest; the ancient temples and monasteries hidden on the heights where the fighting monks of Buddha used to assemble their bands to raid the capital; the basket lunch beside a cold streamlet in a glen below the summit; the rapid descent to Lake Biwa, with rapturous views on the way; the boat-ride home on the swift canal, half through a dark tunnel, half in broad evening sunlight, high on the hillside among wild azaleas,—that was a memorable day.

But a single hour in another day stands out as clear. It was when I climbed with a Japanese friend

CAMP-FIRES

to visit the Christian cemetery on the hillside above Nanzen-ji. The only approach is by a steep footpath. Here, with others of like faith, confessed or secret, is buried Joseph Neesima, the father of Doshisha. From this quiet hillside no doubt he often looked down upon the great city spread out below him, and, like his Master, longed and yearned for its peace. Here he sleeps quietly, while his work goes on.

TO THE CITY OF LANTERNS

This was a roundabout journey which we made with a Japanese friend and scholar, Doctor Harada, as our genial comrade to guide us in the ways of Japanese inns and explain things seen and heard on the road.

First we spent a day and night in Yamada-Isé, visiting the two chief shrines of the Shinto religion. Like almost all sacred places in Japan they have a splendid natural setting.

Unlike Buddhist temples, however, the Shinto shrines are very simple, even austere. Built of plain wood, completely renewed every twenty years, without painting or ornament (except some brass fastenings with crests), they are distinguished by primitive features of their architecture, such as

JAPONICA

the crossing of the end-rafters, which project above the roof like the poles of a wigwam. In the centre of the inner shrine hangs a mirror, the symbol of Amaterasu, the sun-goddess, worshipped as the ancestor of the first Mikado and of the pure Japanese race.

Shintoism is the old national religion of Japan, though there are many more Buddhists than Shintoists, and the two faiths have been strangely crossed. The core of Shinto is ancestor-worship and patriotism. Mr. Hamaguchi said to me one night: "In China they worship their ancestors dead. In Japan we worship our ancestors through our children. Suppose you want to move graveyard to make way for needed railroad. Chinese say, 'Never, our ancestors forbid!' Japanese say, 'Yes, move carefully, with reverence; railroad good for our children.'"

You will usually find chickens kept at Shinto shrines, because of the cock that crows to make the sun rise.

Next we went to Toba, a picturesque seashore town, known for its ship-builders, fishermen, and women pearl-divers. We took two of the divers, plump, good-humored little creatures, out to the fishing-grounds. They put on white caps and huge water-goggles, stood up and dropped their kimonos, and then slipped quietly overboard in their white cotton shirts and drawers, taking their floating tubs with them. After a little wheezing and many curious noises, they gave a sharp, indrawn whistle, turned over, and went down like small white seals. They brought up no pearls, but many lobsters, starfish, sea-urchins, and other marine curios. The best pearl-fishing is at Mikimoto's place, a few miles farther along the coast.

In the afternoon we climbed Weather Hill and had a view finer than that from Pemetic on Mt. Desert: eastward, Isé Bay and the swarm of islands and the blue Pacific; westward, a far-rolling sea of wild mountains and forests.

Our last point was Gifu, the city of lanterns. Here they make delicious persimmon *confitures*, delicate silk crape, the strongest paper in the world, fans, umbrellas, and paper lanterns light as soap-bubbles and lovely as campanula bells. We stayed at the "Well of Jewels Inn," and went out at night to see the celebrated cormorant fishing, a craft which has been practised here for more than ten centuries by the same families of fishermen.

JAPONICA

The moon was rising over the mountains. The swift, clear river ran half glittering and half dark. Our barge was covered with an awning and lit with lanterns. We poled two or three miles up the river and found five other lanterned barges waiting beside a gravelly bank between two rapids. I began to think it would be a "tourist show," a fake.

But a little before ten o'clock we saw moving lights up the river. Six fishing-boats came sweeping down with the current, an iron cresset full of blazing pine-knots projecting from the bow of each. We joined one of them and drifted with it.

In front stood the master fisherman, a tall, bronzed youth, naked to the waist, with a long skirt of straw girt about his loins. The ungainly cormorants,—black bodies, white throats, and hooked bills,—stood along the gunwale, six on a side. A ring of fibre around the lower part of the neck prevents the bird from swallowing fish irrecoverably, and a fibre rein twelve feet long serves to guide and retrieve him. The fisherman pushes the team off in order, the captain last. Then they dive, swim under water with feet and wings, dart hither and thither ahead of the boat, come up again and again with a five or six inch trout held crosswise in the bill, gulp it down, dive again, and keep on till their pouches are full. Then the master, clucking and whistling to his team, lifts one bird after another to the gunwale, taps him on the throat to make him give up his catch, and drops him over once more.

So we drifted on with splashing, shouting, singing, the torches flaring, the birds eager and skilful, the master deft and imperturbable, until we came to the end of the fishing-grounds. Then the birds had their collars taken off and were plentifully fed with the smaller fishes, and we all went home. The catch that night must have run well up in the thousands. We had some the next morning for breakfast,—delicious. Paula said,—well, no matter what she said. They were perfectly good pink fish.

TOKYO REVISITED

Our second week in Tokyo was more serious and joyful than the first. The sun was shining, the air revived. There were social engagements of a real pleasure. A snug tiffin with Secretary Hofer in his new bachelor house; a fine banquet (with theatrical entertainment), given me by six of my former Japanese students at Princeton, in the Maple Club;

JAPONICA

an academic luncheon presided over by Baron Yamagawa, President of the Imperial University, in the Botanical Gardens; a delightful, friendly feast made for us by Madame Yukio Ozaki (wife of the eloquent parliamentary leader, and author of those delightful English volumes, "The Japanese Fairy Book" and "Romances of Old Japan"), at the "Inn of Ten Thousand Pines," by the Sumidagawa; a brilliant dinner with Mrs. Charles Burnett, a gifted American lady who lives very close to the heart of Japan, and whose charm brought to meet us a choice group of scholars and statesmen, men of letters and affairs.

In such company one has glimpses of what Japan really desires and seeks. I am convinced that it is not war, but peaceful, orderly development, and that Japan is the natural leader for this task in the Far East.

There were also academic engagements which involved work. A lecture at Waseda University, founded by Japan's "grand old man," the Marquis Okuma; an address at the fortieth anniversary of the Tokyo Y. M. C. A.; two lectures at the Imperial University, the first to be given on the "House Foundation"; a luncheon and lecture at the Woman's University, where we had a hearty welcome from the president and all the staff and students.

The attitude of the Japanese toward education is fine. In the public schools the enrolment and attendance are 95 per cent. You see the well-trained children on excursions with their teachers everywhere, learning to see and know Japan first. In the universities the eagerness for knowledge is keen, —so keen that perhaps it sometimes turns its own edge. Know-it-all is a good dog, but Know-it-well is a better.

The Japanese, in fact, have many of the American virtues,—and faults. To think or talk of them as "brown monkeys" is distinctly asinine. They have an ancient civilization; a wonderful art and literature; a unified race whose spirit has never been broken by foreign conquest or domination; a habit of industry and great gifts of manual skill; endurance, ambition, versatility, and a sensitive temper. They laugh much, love their numerous and delightful children, and have a firm and passionate faith in the future of their country. They are almost as political-minded as Americans, and quite as honest as any other commercial people.

JAPONICA

One word more. What about the Pacific Coast and Japanese Immigration?

Only this!

It is a difficult question. Within limits, I think the Pacific Coasters must settle it for themselves. If they do not want Japanese labor they need not have it. If they want it they must treat it on the principle of "the square deal."

The Californians must remember that the Pacific has two Coasts. The friendly co-operation of Great Britain, the United States, and Japan is essential to peace and order in the Far East, where our nation has some possessions and many interests. And the natural leader in the Far East is Japan, because she has what China lacks, the instinct of self-organization.

XIII

INTERLUDES ON THE KOTO

I

THE RED BRIDGE AT NIKKO

OVER the hurrying torrent of Daiya-gawa,
Calmly I bend my bow of beauty,
Curving from pillar to pillar of granite,
Tranquil in the pride of perfection,—
I am the Queen-rose of all bridges.

I tremble not with the fury of the current;
The turbulent river cannot reflect me,
Nor carry away my lovely image.

Holy and proud, I am often lonely,
When I hear on the common bridge below me
The pattering feet of people going to and fro,
And the merry laughter of little children.

Come in the night, you wild young boy,
And leave me not untrodden.

INTERLUDES

II

CANDELABRA

I LOVE the wonder-working fingers
Of Springtime in Japan!
She weaves a priestly robe of green for Nature,
And broiders it with white and rose and gold.
She lifts the veil of snow
From the beautiful mountain-shoulders,
She fills the holy places of the forest
With psalms and canticles of praise.
Incense of fragrant leaves and blossoms
Floats from her footsteps in the temple.

Where are the candelabra for the altar?
Behold, the fingers of Springtime have prepared them!
She has wrought silently in the midnight;
Bending the dark bronze boughs of the pine-trees
Outward and upward in lines of beauty.
On the tips of all the branches, straight and slender,
Silvery candles are set in millions,—
Every one standing upright,
Every one touched with the white flame of life!

CAMP-FIRES

III

THE REPOSE OF NARA

On the knees of the ancient mountains
Guarding the old Yamato plain,
Weary of long war and tumult,
Beautiful Nara climbed up to rest.

The green *sugi* and red-bodied *hinoki*
Shelter her temples with curving branches:
April heaps white blossoms among them,
October lights them with lanterns of a million
    maples.

Droves of dappled deer find sanctuary in Nara;
Processions of pilgrims and singing school children
Wander and wonder through her groves,
While the great bell of Buddha
Booms the passing hours of peace.

Last of all come the refugees of Russia,
Flying from the fury of the Red Terror.
Dai Nippon, whom they once despised and hated,
Welcomes them to the repose of Nara.
They are like people walking in their sleep;
Happy, if in this dream they find truth!

INTERLUDES

IV

PROMISE-TIME

If Springtime were the only time
    It would not be so dear,—
The budding-time, the mating-time,
    The promise-time o' the year.
But Summer comes with ripening heat,
And Autumn with her wine-stained feet,
And Winter to his fireside seat
    Doth cheerily call:

Yet still the dearest time of all,
Is the time when nothing is complete,—
The time when hope and longing meet,—
    The promise-time o' the year.

V

MALGRÉ CELA

Never Summer fair as Spring foretold,
Never Autumn rich as Summer willed it,
Never Winter gleaned all Autumn's gold,
Never Spring so late that Winter killed it.

VI

WILD AZALEAS

When the bloom of the cherry is gone from the gardens
And all their white flower-drifts have melted away,
Then the wild azaleas begin to flow down the hillsides,—
Rivers of rose through the morning-misty woodland,
Pools of tranquil flame under the evergreen-trees.

VII

THE SPIRIT OF JAPAN

While the broad-boughed pine braves the ocean gale,
And the bamboo bends to the breath of the vale,
And the cherry dazzles the April air
With a snow of beauty everywhere,—
The Yamato spirit shall endure,
In beauty, grace, and strength secure.

XIV

SUICIDAL TENDENCIES IN DEMOCRACY

DEMOCRACY is a word variously employed. It signifies a government, a theory, a way of living, and (like Boston) a state of mind. In the United States of America it is also used, and capitalized, to denote one of the two political parties which alternately control and criticise the conduct of the state. With this last meaning the present essay does not deal.

Toward the four other significations of democracy I stand thus. As a state of mind it is wholesome: as a way of living it is convenient, although not always the most comfortable: as a theory it is admirable with mild reservations: as a mode of government it is the most promising yet devised by man.

This is not as much as to say that it is always possible or even desirable for all nations at all stages of their growth. What has been written by Rudyard

Kipling of the Bandar-log or commonwealth of monkeys is pertinent also to the Boob-rah or régime of the ignorant by force of numbers.

But granting a moderate degree of self-knowledge as a preparative for self-determination, and a reasonable consent to those natural and moral laws which cannot be altered by popular vote, probably democracy offers more to man than any other way of regulating his common affairs.

It is costly in discussion and debate; but by way of recompense it promotes general intelligence and the most Christian virtue of patience. It is subject to errors; but it has the merit of bringing home the responsibility to those who make the mistakes; for where all decide, all must share the consequences.

Under a rule in which you yourself partake, weak complaining is a form of self-reproach, violence is treason, and the only wisdom of the discontented lies in the continued effort to bring the majority to a better choice. Thus democracy, rightly considered, has in itself something bracing, salutary, and educative.

"Government of the people, by the people, for the people," as Lincoln ennobled it in his imperishable phrase, has a superior quality in its ideal of

TENDENCIES IN DEMOCRACY

perfection. Even in its imperfection, (and as yet the world has seen no more,) it outranks the other methods of government by its ultimate intention of appeal to reason and the right mind in man.

Thus avowing my democratic convictions, and thanking God that he has cast my lot under a government which derives its just powers from the consent of the governed, I feel bound, (and at liberty,) to confess my hesitations and doubts concerning the modern presentation of democracy as a substitute for religion.

It is a good thing, no doubt: but not so good as all that. It has the defects of its qualities. Its possibilities carry its perils. Subject to the infirmities of its makers, it needs a corrective and a guide. It is as wise and just as mankind,—no more.

Perhaps they are right who say that it has more of wisdom and justice than any one man can ever have. But even that collective sum is not enough. For human wisdom has its sharp enclosing ring; and when we pass that, we do but find another horizon. Human justice has a twist in it, being warped unconsciously by our fond blindness to our own blame, and our failure to feel the needs which may explain, if not excuse, the faults of others.

This double defect is as common in juries as in judges.

To praise democracy overmuch is to invite a scrutiny of its mistakes. To trust it beyond its ability to perform is to court the loss of all our confidence.

Do not overload the ship which carries your hope. *Vox populi, vox dei*, says the proverb. Yes, but what god is it that thus speaks? An idol of the market-place, or the True and Only?

You might think that the new religion proposed by Auguste Comte,—*Culte systématique de l'Humanité*,—would have been popular. Not so! For the enthusiasm of the multitude for itself, though violent for a time, is transitory. The hot fit passes into the cold.

The crowd, when not hypnotized by the spellbinder, or inflamed by the demagogue, mistrusts itself even more than the philosopher who knows the *common sense* which lives within its limitations.

The man in the crowd, pressed and incommoded, is conscious mainly of the deficiencies of his too near neighbor, and whispers to himself, "Am I to be governed by the likes of you?"

You may often hear one say, in mock-modest

TENDENCIES IN DEMOCRACY

self-depreciation, that he belongs to the rank and file. But in his heart he does not place himself entirely there. He thinks he is a little different, stands somewhat apart, a bit higher.

This is why even popular writers do not fear to abuse the multitude, to pour scorn upon it, to buffet it with hard words. They know that none of their readers will take offense, because none will think that he really belongs to the multitude.

Thus Emerson, high-handed republican that he was, wrote in his "Considerations by the Way": "Leave this hypocritical prating about the masses. Masses are rude, lame, unmade, pernicious in their demands and influence, and need not to be flattered, but to be schooled. I wish not to concede anything to them, but to tame, drill, divide, and break them up, and draw individuals out of them. The worst of charity is, that the lives you are asked to preserve are not worth preserving. Masses! the calamity is masses. I do not wish any mass at all, but honest men only, lovely, sweet, accomplished women only, and no shovel-handed, narrow-brained, gin-drinking million stockingers or lazzaroni at all. If government knew how, I should like to see it check, not multiply the population. When it reaches its true law of action, every man that is born will be hailed as essential. Away with this hurrah of masses, and let us have the considerate vote of single men spoken on their honor and their conscience. In old Egypt, it was established law, that the vote of a prophet be reckoned equal to a hundred hands. I think it was much underestimated. 'Clay and clay differ in dignity,' as we find by our preferences every day. What a vicious practice is this of our politicians at Washington pairing off! as if one man who votes wrong, going away, could excuse you, who mean to vote right, for going away; or as if your presence did not tell in more ways than in your vote. Suppose the three hundred heroes of Thermopylæ had paired off with three hundred Persians; would it have been all the same to Greece, and to history?"

Now whether this be an example of what George Meredith calls a "rough truth" or not, I cannot say; but it is certainly a specimen of plain discourse. One would like to know after what election in Massachusetts Emerson wrote it, or whether it was conceived after a confabulation with Carlyle in his "Ercles' vein."

But at one point,—the last,—Emerson leaves his

TENDENCIES IN DEMOCRACY

belaboring of the unconscious masses, and turns to thwack a far more sensitive class, the politicians. And that, forsooth, on the score of their old-established, highly honored, and generally practised custom of pairing off! Here is candor to the verge of rashness! I reckon, calculate, and guess the sage of Concord heard from his representatives at Washington about that rude assault. Thus I hear them talk:

'Shall not a weary Congressman or Senator pair off when he has important business of his own to attend to, and when a vote on one side practically cancels and annuls a vote on the other? Instead of being blamed, should he not rather be praised for having taken the pains to arrange a pair before forsaking the high halls of republican council? Is not this a pestilent idealist who ventures to set up a higher standard of duty than the convenience or interest of the men who have been honored, and so to speak promoted to a kind of nobility, by the people's choice?'

A specious defense! Yet Emerson was right. The point he makes against the pairing politicians is that their mating of opposites is productive of mere negation; it is a barren match. And this, mark you, because it proceeds upon the false assumption that voting is the highest if not the sole function of man in a democratic state, and that all votes are equal, not only in the numerical count, but also in worth and significance.

This assumption, if granted, would be fatal to true democracy. It would level down, not up; render the appeal to reason and the right mind nugatory; and consecrate the Teller as High-Priest of the God of Numbers.

Yet it is precisely the democratic state that seems to breed this self-destroying fallacy most frequently and to its own hurt. *One man, one vote*, is the modern "slogan." (Silly word, beloved by advertisers of ready-made clothing and cosmetics, I use thee in derision!) As a protest against proved inequities of suffrage, like plural voting and the disfranchising of women on the ground of sex, the saying has its portion of truth. But push it beyond the mark, infer from it that, because the privilege of voting works best when equally conferred on all citizens, therefore all citizens and all their votes have an equal vital value, and you propagate an absurdity which not even the rugged digestion of democracy can endure.

TENDENCIES IN DEMOCRACY

In old Calvinton, when I was young, we had a professor who was a saint, a sage, and a joy to the heart. Every one in the town knew and loved him. As he rode along the main street in his little one-horse carryall on election day, we would say, "There goes the old Doctor to vote the Republicratic ticket." When he had deposited his ballot, he would come out, climb into the back seat of the wagon, and smilingly hold the reins, while his Irish coachman went in to exercise the proud privilege of suffrage. As Pat emerged from the polls, he would grin, and whisper behind the back of his hand to the bystanders, "Begorrah, oi've just nulligated ould Docther's vote!" But had Pat done as much as that? Neither he himself nor the laughing bystanders really thought so. There was something in the example of the wise old Doctor faithfully performing a simple duty of citizenship that counted far beyond the ballot he had dropped in the box. It could not be equalled save by a man of equal wisdom and character.

Why, then, should those who prefer a democratic form of government and believe in *one man, one vote*, as the best means of securing it, surcharge their faith with inferences which are manifestly false;

like the dogma that all men have equal worth and influence because they have an equal right to "life, liberty and the pursuit of happiness." The founders of our republic neither held nor practised that inane creed.

Such an excessive orthodoxy has all the vices of a heresy. The preaching of it, either in serious fanaticism or for campaign purposes, injures and imperils the republic. It is, in effect, an illustration of the theme which I have been meditating by this month's autumnal camp-fire,—suicidal tendencies in democracy.

By this phrase I do not mean carefully matured purposes of self-destruction; nor even sudden impulses and resolves which have that end clearly in view as a risk. They do not fall under either head of Blackstone's definition of *felo de se* as one who "deliberately puts an end to his own existence, or commits any unlawful act the consequence of which is his own death."

The tendencies of which I speak are marked by a lack of deliberation. Nor can they be called unlawful acts, since the body which commits them has authority to make them legal. They have for the most part the quality of unconscious self-betrayal

TENDENCIES IN DEMOCRACY

and inconsistent action,—the harboring of views and the forming of habits which carry seeds of decay and presages of dissolution for the democratic state. And these are at their worst, most secret and perilous, precisely in those times and countries where the democratic theory is presented as a substitute for religion, and the ancient heresy that "the king can do no wrong" is twisted to read "the sovereign people can make no mistakes."

This dogma of popular infallibility goes directly in the teeth of experience, and cancels that wise and needful maxim of the Hebrew commonwealth, "Thou shalt not follow a multitude to do evil."

A thoughtful consideration of the self-begotten errors and morbific propensities which brought about the downfall of such democracy as existed in Athens, in republican Rome, in revolutionary France, and more recently, for a few months, in unhappy Russia, dreaming of freedom and walking straight into the ditch of Soviet slavery,—such a study would yield matter for a book of profitable warnings. But for our present purpose of a camp-fire talk, (with side-reference to guide-posts,) there is no need to go so far back or afield. There are plenty of small instances and significant illustrations close at hand in these States, where democracy has found its greatest opportunity.

THE REFERENDUM HABIT

What shall we say, for instance, of the tendency to supersede the considerate processes of representative government by submitting complicated questions which require long thought and enlightened judgment, to the direct, immediate yes-or-no vote of the masses? Calling it a referendum does not alter its nature. It is a demand upon the multitude for what the multitude has not got and cannot deliver,—expert knowledge on a variety of subjects and a careful solution of intricate problems. Or else it is an attempt to get rid of the burden of responsibility by throwing it upon the untrained shoulders of the people.

A California woman has told in a recent magazine the unconsciously pathetic story of her first experience at the polls in her glorious native State. She was confronted, a few weeks before the election, with a vast, portentous referendum which summoned her to stand and deliver her judgment on forty-two points of public policy. (I think that was the number, but a few more or less would make no difference.) This conscientious and heroic woman shivered, studied, struggled, did her best to perform her enormous duty in a more than manful way. But at the end she was rather in the dark as to just what she had done, and the joy of her first vote was troubled by spasms of dubiety.

Lowell wrote: "Direct intervention of the people in their own affairs is not of the essence of democracy"; and further: "The founders of our democracy put as many obstacles as they could contrive, not in the way of the people's will, but of their whim." That is sound doctrine.

Real reform and progress in politics must be accomplished bit by bit. Sudden revolutions may succeed, but do not prosper.

To change personnel, machinery, and methods in a factory at one sweep, is usually fatal. New men, machines, and processes, must be brought in by degrees. It is only in her destructive work that Nature operates by the catastrophic method.

The referendum, no doubt, has its use and justification in certain cases,—in matters which have been long discussed and are generally understood, —in questions which are clear and definite and admit of a categorical answer,—will you or won't you have it so? Even then, I think it takes its best form in the choice of representatives who stand definitely on one side or the other of the clear question at issue.

The formation of the indiscriminate, indolent, universal referendum habit in a democracy looks to me like a vice with suicidal tendency.

LEGIMANIA

Another bad habit which seems to endanger the security, or at least the sound health of a democracy, is the propensity to make too many laws on too many subjects.

Somewhere in my filing-cabinet I have the statistics in regard to the number of laws enacted by the legislatures of New York, California, and other States, in a single recent year. It runs well up into the thousands; and if you add to it the Acts of Congress passed in the same time, you have a sum total which represents a solemn revel of legimania.

'Tis as if a doctor should seek to win respect and confidence by the extraordinary number of his prescriptions, or a schoolmaster to establish discipline

TENDENCIES IN DEMOCRACY

by multiplying his rules. The thing cannot be done in that way.

Doubtless some of these laws are wise and needful. Probably most of them are well meant. They have a good heart, as the saying goes. It is in the head they are lacking. And so in practice many of them produce either no effect at all, or the contrary of what was intended.

Not even the Puritan Fathers in their palmiest days went as far in sumptuary legislation as some of our modern regulators would have us go.

Of old, men were rebuked by the Divine Master for asking continually, "What shall we eat, and what shall we drink, and wherewithal shall we be clothed?" Nowadays it seems to be no reproach to be asking continually, "What food and drink and raiment shall we permit our neighbors to use?"

"You can never make men virtuous by legislation," said the Bromidian Philosopher. "Perhaps not," replied the Acidulous Reformer, "but I can make them—uncomfortable."

It is a historic fact that the American form of government has as its basis and its aim, liberty,— the largest amount of liberty in action for the individual that is consistent with a due regard for the liberties of others. To abandon that basis is to impair the stability of the republic: to renounce that aim is to deprive democracy of one of its main appeals to the common sense of mankind.

As few rules as possible, but those well enforced: that is the régime of wisdom and strength.

You can never secure by popular vote that which is not supported by public opinion.

The tyranny of a meddlesome majority is as obnoxious as the interference of a capricious king.

The democracy that goes beyond its duty of abating public nuisances and protecting public health, to indulge its illusion of omnipotence by regulating private affairs, weakens its own power by overstraining it.

The craze for superlegislation in a democratic state has a suicidal aspect. It undermines authority, lessens respect, and begets a brood of resentful evasions under the smooth apron of hypocritical compliance.

FICKLENESS

We expect the masses to be fickle, and they seldom disappoint us. But when that frivolity of

TENDENCIES IN DEMOCRACY

mind takes a violent form and swings to the alternate "falsehood of extremes," it becomes dangerous to the state.

Republics are always looking for heroes and always pulling them down. How many Washingtons and Lincolns has America discovered, only to revile them afterward as would-be Cæsars! A study of newspaper cartoons from the Jacksonian period to the present would show the head of many a good and faithful servant of his country encircled with the mocking laurels of imperial ambition.

It is a bad habit of democracy to oscillate between adoration and abuse. When Admiral Dewey came home from his famous victory at Manila Bay, nothing was too good for him; he was a second Nelson, the savior of his country, worthy of the highest place. But a few months later, when he quite properly made his wife a wedding present of the house in Washington which the public had given to him, (thinking, honest man, that as he and she were one, the sharing of the gift was natural,) the fickle populace could find nothing too bad to say of him. He could not have been elected to a seat in the House of Representatives, to say nothing of the Presidential Chair. Yet he remained just

CAMP-FIRES

what he always was, a great, quiet, naval commander.

Death has a way of silencing these violent reactions in the people. It is only a few among the journalists who cherish the malice of their oppugnancies and pursue the men whom they have scorned into the grave. For the public at large, the vanishing of the contestant from the field of partisan strife, means a calmer and deeper vision of the man and his services. I know more than one New York clubman who used to swear profanely at the mere mention of Roosevelt's name while he was alive, who walked among the mourners at his funeral when that strong and valiant soul was gone.

Most assuredly this habit in democracy of first blindly adoring and then cruelly abusing its public men while they are in life is a suicidal trait. The danger of it is twofold.

Some day an idol of the public may come along who is really a Napoleon or a Lenin in disguise; and then,—good-by, democracy. That is one danger.

The other is quite the reverse. Many a day the republic imperils the usefulness of a noble servant, cripples him or maims him for the time, by the ex-

TENDENCIES IN DEMOCRACY

travagance of partisan scorn and vituperation. This also is madness and folly, vanity and a striving after wind.

Even worse than fickleness in regard to heroes is the democratic propensity to shift and veer on matters of public policy. It is a habit of minor politicians to maintain their leadership by following what looks like the crowd.

I remember a certain President of whom it was often said that he had his ear to the ground. "Watch him closely," a shrewd critic said to me, "and before long you'll see dust on the other ear."

What does it signify when at a certain time there is general enthusiasm in America for a league of nations to maintain peace and the leaders of both parties cry out that it is the hope of the world, and then, two years later, the enthusiasm has cooled and half of the leaders exclaim that such an idea is preposterous, impossible, a menace to the world, and to the United States in particular? This also is vanity and a striving after wind.

What does it signify when at one time the Monroe Doctrine is extolled as the Palladium of our safety, and at another time the proposal to give it a recognized standing in international law is refused with mockery? when men claim effusively that the United States is now a world-power, and soon afterward shout "What do we care for Abroad?" This also is vanity and a striving after wind.

A foolish inconsistency may be "the hobgoblin of little minds," as Emerson said. But for a great democracy it is something worse than that. It is a bar to a sober and settled foreign policy, and a disturber of domestic order and progress. It makes the pomp of politics ridiculous, and exposes the republic to that kind of laughter among the nations which is a warning of trouble. It needs correcting, either by our sense of humor, or by our sense of honor.

SCORN OF KNOWLEDGE

There are other self-destroying propensities in a democratic state which we might well consider and discuss if there were time. But the camp-fire wanes; and before the logs break apart and fall, we must give a thought to the most dangerous tendency of all,—contempt of learning for its own sake, scorn of that elemental knowledge which is the basis of character, and frivolous neglect of popular education.

TENDENCIES IN DEMOCRACY

But is not America free from that defect? Are not Americans the best-educated people in the world? They are not. And the worst of it is, they think they are.

In the matter of universities and professional schools we have done astonishingly well, as Bryce remarked, (to our great satisfaction,) in his excellent book on *The American Commonwealth*. Yet even in this respect, if we may take the testimony of recent home-made and much-praised books on American college life, there is much to be desired in the way of manners, morals, and mental culture among the average frequenters of what we call our higher institutions of learning. To speak frankly, these pictures do not cheer, though they may inebriate.

But when we turn to the broader field and look at the general condition and actual results of popular education in these States, the view is dismal. It would be laughable if it were not appalling. Half a dozen small European states, Canada, Australia, New Zealand, and Japan are all ahead of America in school attendance and literacy. The selective draft of 1917 uncovered the ugly fact that about twenty-five per cent of the men of America between

CAMP-FIRES

eighteen and thirty-five years of age are unable to read a newspaper or write a letter. Ten per cent cannot write their own names. There are seven and a half million people in the United States over sixteen years old who can neither read nor write English or any other language.

Negroes, you say, or ignorant foreigners! If that were so, would it make the case any better, since these are actual or potential voters, our future masters? But in fact more than half of these untaught sovereigns of the state are white, and nearly one-third of them are white Americans, home-born and home-bred.

What was democracy thinking of when it suffered this perilous bulk of ignorance to grow within its own body? Are the national institutions in which we take such a just and honorable pride safe in the hands of men and women whose minds are left in darkness and whose moral training is committed to chance or charity, while we use their bodies to work our farms, dig our ditches, build our railways, and run our factories?

We are breeding a Helot class of our own flesh and blood. We are ignoring the rightful claim of every citizen to be prepared for the duties which

TENDENCIES IN DEMOCRACY

the state lays upon him. We are debasing the human currency of the republic. We are laying unbaked bricks in our foundations and building our walls with untempered mortar. We are heaping up at the doors of our own temple piles of tinder and quick-flaming fuel, ready for the torch of the anarchist or the insidious slow-match of the cunning usurper. We are recruiting the sullen armies of ignorant unrest;

> For every soul denied the right to grow
> Beneath the flag, will be its secret foe.

But who denies that right? Democracy denies it, by neglect and parsimony, by a careless disregard of the crying needs of popular education.

But is not our public-school system open to all? It is; but the door is narrow, and few there be that find it,—few, I mean, of those who need it most. For the children of the rich, the well-to-do, the moderately comfortable, the provision of schools is ample. It is the children of the poor who suffer and go in want.

In the great city of New York last year one hundred thousand poor children were deprived of schooling. And why? Because there were no teachers

CAMP-FIRES

to instruct them. And again, why? Because the pay offered to teachers was too small to keep them alive.

Democracy gives its carpenters, bricklayers, plumbers, and the like, more for their work than it gives to those who have the supreme task of enlightening and training its children. Does not this look as if it cared more for its houses than for its offspring, more for its goods than for its soul?

In the labor-unions of New York (1919) the average yearly wage of skilled workers was $2,496, of unskilled workers $1,664. The wage of teachers was $1,240. Is not this indisputable evidence that scorn of knowledge and silent contempt of education prevail to some extent in America?

Is this safe? Is it true economy to indulge the proletariat and starve the *educariat?* (There may be no such word, but there is such a thing, the whole body of teachers, consecrated to a common task and bound together by mutual dependence for the success of their work.) Is liberty itself secure in a country which boasts of its possession but takes no care for its preservation?

"Freedom, to be desirable," says Stevenson, "involves kindness, wisdom, and all the virtues of

TENDENCIES IN DEMOCRACY

the free." But these do not spring out of the ground by nature. They must be implanted, nurtured, developed, and trained.

Nothing is more difficult to preserve than the true love of freedom in a free country. Being habituated to it, men cease to consider by what sacrifices it was obtained, and by what precautions and safeguards it must be defended.

Liberty itself is the great lesson. And in learning it we need teachers,—the wise, the just, the free of all ages. Most of all we need the help of religion, by which alone the foundations of the state are laid in righteousness, and democracy is saved from its own suicidal tendencies.

Come, let us cover the fire, and so to bed, not forgetting an honest prayer for the country we love best.

XV

A BUNDLE OF LETTERS

MANY unknown correspondents, from all corners of the earth, wrote to the Camp-fire Cogitator while some of these papers were coming out in *Scribner's Magazine*. Almost all of the letters were kind and heartening. Many of them were informing, instructive, full of human interest.

See, here is a little bundle of them,—covered with all sorts of postmarks,—messages from strange cities and far-off wildernesses and lonely farms and ships at sea,—tokens of that hidden friendliness which lies all round us in the world. One came just the other day, by wireless telegraph, from the British Admiral at Bermuda, while I was sailing homeward: "May I say, *So long?*"

Many of the letters were answers to a question in "Firelight Views,"—do you remember?—about the lovely old-fashioned rose with the forgotten name. Here is a sample of these answers, which comes from Elizabethtown in the Adirondacks, and was written

A BUNDLE OF LETTERS

by a lady with whom I played when she was a little girl, but whom I have not seen for more years than it would be polite to number.

"I believe the rose you refer to in the June *Scribner's* is the 'Gold of Ophir,'—a single, or half-double, climbing rose, growing over porches in California when I was there twenty-five years ago. It had a deep yellow heart, shading into rose colors on the edges, and having a curious lavender sheen flickering through the yellow and rose, very lovely.

C. P. H."

Yes, dear lady, that is the rose,—*Gold of Ophir*,—and I'm glad that word about it comes from the friendly mountain-land where you live. But my own first sight of that softly, purely flaming flower was forty-four years ago on a veranda at the "Sand Hills," near Augusta, Georgia. The rose queened it over all the red and white camellias.

One of my most prized letters came from an unknown Canadian soldier, G. J. S., who is now farming in Saskatchewan. A fine little story is quoted from it in the chapter on "Christmas Greens." He signs himself, "Yours to a camp-fire cinder."

CAMP-FIRES

But once in a while a letter arrives which belongs in a different class. Here is a specimen:

"San Francisco, Cal.
Feb. 13, 1921.
"HENRY VAN DYKE, ESQUIRE.
"*Dear Sir:*—

"After reading your article in November 'Scribner's,' (Suicidal Tendencies in Democracy), I am impelled to differ with you, and as criticism is not always distasteful, here you are.

"1. About school teachers:—In this city they have easy hours, paid vacation periods, and then in old age a pension. About 75% are Roman Catholics who would teach the public schools out of existence if they could earn a living at anything else. Recently, though, the Americans asserted themselves, with the result that, by a *narrow majority*, the Irish crowd were beaten.

"2. There is too much education to be had free of cost. Nearly everybody is educated now, with the result that 90% of the graduates spend their young lives looking around for something easy to do. The men who discovered and developed this great state were not college graduates or bookworms.

A BUNDLE OF LETTERS

"3. Democracy—The American brand of Democracy is a farce. Here is an example. By a majority of 65000 votes the people of California voted 'wet.' Immediately thereafter their duly elected representatives met and voted 'dry.' This is a notorious fact, and yet political orators get up and shout about the land of liberty. In a rougher age, or in sane Bolshevist community, the aforesaid legislators would have been hanged or shot. American democracy, I repeat, is a farce, and the talk of representative government is all 'bunk.' Pardon the slang.

"The only thing to do in this democracy is to make as much money as possible and then hide it away securely from the small army of tax-eaters that fattens itself, à la parasite, in every community.

Yours truly,

A Western Spectator."

Now that is an anonymous letter, which is usually a thing of shame. But this one is not at all shameful. It is frank; it is friendly in purpose; it is courteous enough; there is no reason at all why the author should not have put his name to it.

Yet at the end it seems to me to go a little crazy.

What do you think? Read the last sentence. Is not this a graphic illustration of "Suicidal Tendencies in Democracy"?

XVI

CHRISTMAS GREENS

(WRITTEN IN AUTUMN)

"THE time draws near the birth of Christ,"—

you remember, reader, the rest of those lovely cantoes of *In Memoriam*, where the bells of four villages answer each other through the misty night while the wreaths of evergreen are woven with memories and regrets to deck the church and the home in honor of the best of all birthdays.

Once more the Yuletide is near,—near at least to the Slave of the Magazine, though by the dull, prosaic almanac it is still months away. For me it is proximate and pressing. The editor cajoles and threatens: the printer waits at extra wages for overtime: to-morrow will be Christmas and the day after will be New Year; and I must gather the figurative greens to-day, or leave our Christmas Camp-fire without a token of remembrance or a sign of cheer.

CAMP-FIRES

But what a day is this on which I set about my pleasant task! Indian summer at its golden best: the blue of the sky subdued by a silvery haze to the tint of turquoise, faintly luminous: the verdure of the woodlands, ripened and dulled a little by the August heat, now shot through with the first rich threads of autumnal glory: the mountains growing higher and more aerial, as they recede in the light mist, until they change into bastions of amethyst: the deep blue of the open sea ever deepening far away, while the white flower of foam above the hidden reef expands and closes with every passing wave,—a mystic lily on a sleeper's breast.

From every orchard the smell of ripening apples comes out to us, and from the tangled thicket we catch the odor of fox-grapes, waiting for the frost to sweeten them. Wild asters and goldenrod adorn the wayside; gentians bloom in secret places. The little birds have assembled their silent companies for southward flight. But they are loath to leave their summer haunts, and if we go warily through the wood, they will flock around us suddenly, fluttering through the coppice in search of food, flitting from branch to branch of the dark firs, lisping, calling, whispering *sotto voce*, no doubt talking over

CHRISTMAS GREENS

their plans for the long journey to Central America.

All round us as we walk through this ephemeral beauty, the more enduring growths which are to serve for adornment in our homes at the midwinter festival are visible and suggestive to the inward eye which looks far ahead. Here the young spruces and balsam-firs, shapely and symmetrical pyramids of absolute green, are standing by thousands in the open places,—regiments of Christmas-trees! Here

> "The ground-pine trails its pretty wreath
> Running over the club-moss burrs,"

ready to be twined into garlands or long festoons. Here the glistening, prickly holly lights its dark foliage with red berries; and the ground-hemlock hides its delicate coral fruit like drops of translucent wax under its spreading branches; and the climbing bittersweet curls back its orange pods to show the scarlet-covered seeds within; and the pale-green mistletoe,—not just here perhaps, but a little farther south,—prepares its pearly berries to sanction kisses yet unkissed.

Nature in her lavish way provides beauty for every season: flowers that fade and vanish as the summer goes: gold and crimson leaves that fall as the autumn wanes: and evergreens that will stay with us in rich and sober loveliness when

> "Full knee-deep lies the winter snow,
> And the winter winds are wearily sighing."

All these things are given us to enjoy. They are best in the place where nature put them, out-of-doors: but a little of each and all we may rightly take, if we will, to deck our dwellings, if for no other purpose than to be a fragrant reminder that we are more akin to nature than to our houses.

Shall we grieve, then, at the thought that some of these pretty, wild, growing things will be cut and gathered for Christmas greens? Not I,—if the cutting and gathering are wisely done, with kindly forethought of the coming generations, so that no sort of harmless vine or amiable tree shall be exterminated from the earth.

Let us not spoil our love of nature with a sickly affection. There are enough evergreen things in our country to provide a sign of Christmas for every house and church in it. To gather them prudently is to practise a kind of forestry. After all, one can think of no fairer way for a little fir-tree to complete its life than by becoming for a while the

CHRISTMAS GREENS

sparkling centre of a circle of human joy,—a Christmas-tree! If your imagination must endow the little fir with feelings, why not give it this fine emotion of ending in glory?

I confess myself out of sympathy with those writers who complain that they must write their Christmas stories in midsummer and their August fiction in midwinter. Incongruous it may seem, but such incongruity is of the very warp and woof of life.

Always we are looking backward and forward while we live the passing hour. Every true pleasure hath in it an extract of the past and a tincture of the future.

I think it was that great artist John La Farge who said "all drawing of the things we see is an exercise of memory, and the things we have seen enter into it." The springs of poetry, Wordsworth found, have their origin in "emotion recollected in tranquillity." This is true of noble sorrow as of pure joy. There is not one little delight that comes to us without a flavor of reminder. When we lie on a bed of balsam boughs in the forest we dream of a Christmas-tree. When we enter the room where the gift-laden, candle-lighted tree waits for the

CAMP-FIRES

children, the very smell of it carries us away to camp in the greenwood.

You may call this "sentimental," if you will, Brother Gradgrind, and scoff at it in your sour, self-satisfied way. But it is by this thread that our personalities are held together. If you have it not, as you boast, that is probably why you are a person so little to be envied, a thing of shreds and patches, but no man.

There is no present reality for us humans, without memory and hope. Lose the first, and you are dead; lose the second, and you are buried. But in Christmas, as truly as in Easter, if we come to it in the spirit, there is a power of resurrection.

The custom of adorning our houses and places of worship at this season with green tokens from the winter woods came down to us, no doubt, from heathen ancestors who dwelt, as we do, in what is ironically called the north temperate zone. It was partly a tribute to unknown gods, and partly an expression of man's wish to make himself comfortable and even merry in the teeth of the rudest weather.

In the tropics, of course, there would be no call for this defiance of the frost. And in the southern

CHRISTMAS GREENS

hemisphere the seasons would be reversed; instead of Christmas greens there would be a festival of flowers out-of-doors. There must be something charming in that; yet those who have tasted the ruder and more bracing joys of a northern Christmas always hone for them, and cannot be comforted with palms and pomegranates. Shakespeare, in *Love's Labor's Lost*, makes Biron say,

"At Christmas I no more desire a rose,
Than wish a snow in May's new-fangled shows."

Some hold that the decking of houses with green branches in December originated among the Druids, and was a pious provision for the poor sylvan spirits,—elves and fays and good goblins,—who needed a shelter from the nipping cold. That may be what the Druids told the people; but I think natural inclination and a love of beauty had a good deal to do with it.

Religious customs are most easily accepted when they fit in with human desires.

Holly with its bright sheen and vivid color was the symbol of mirth and good cheer. Ivy was sacred to Bacchus, and hung over the door of wine-shops; yet if I mistake not there was also an ancient tradition that while it invited to drinking it was a talisman against drunkenness,—a most considerate and helpful arrangement! Laurel and bay were signs of honor and festivity.

Mistletoe was the most weird and magical of all the Christmas greens, feared a little because of its association with druidical sacrifices, yet loved a good deal for its modern uses. They say that in the olden time it was admitted in the Yuletide decoration of houses, but not of churches. Yet one of the antiquarians tells us that in the eighteenth century, in York Cathedral, it was the custom on Christmas Eve to carry a branch of mistletoe to the high altar and "proclaim a public and universal liberty, pardon, and freedom to all sorts of inferior and even wicked people at the gates of the city toward the four quarters of heaven."

Here we find, perhaps, a hint of that liberty of osculation with which the homely plant is now connected. And this, again, we may dimly trace back to the Scandinavian myth. For the arrow with which the rascally Loki tricked the blind Höder into killing Baldur the beautiful, was made of mistletoe. When the fatal shaft was plucked out, the mistletoe was given into the keeping of Freya, the

CHRISTMAS GREENS

love-goddess; and henceforth on every one who passes beneath it she bestows a kiss,—a right pleasant legend with a happy ending! Yet after all, if Freya,—well, I will say no more than this, *if* Freya!

There is a quaint reference on this point in Hawthorne's "English Note-Books," under date of December 26, 1855. He was then American Consul at Liverpool living in the cosey boarding-house of Mrs. Blodgett. "On Christmas Eve and yesterday," he says, "there were branches of mistletoe hanging in several parts of the house, in the kitchen, the entries, the parlor, and the smoking-room,—suspended from the gas-fittings. The maids of the house did their utmost to entrap the gentlemen boarders, old and young, under the privileged places, and there to kiss them, after which they were expected to pay a shilling. It is very queer, being customarily so respectful, that they should assume this license now, absolutely trying to pull the gentlemen into the kitchen by main force, and kissing the harder and more abundantly the more they were resisted. A little rosy-cheeked Scotch lass—at other times very modest—was the most active in this business. *I doubt whether any gentleman but myself escaped.* [Italics mine.] I heard old **Mr. S——** parleying with the maids last evening and pleading his age; but he seems to have met with no mercy, for there was a sound of prodigious smacking immediately afterwards. **J——** was assaulted, and fought most vigorously; but was outrageously kissed—receiving some scratches, moreover, in the conflict. The mistletoe has white wax-looking berries, and dull green leaves, with a parasitical stem."

Oh, Mr. Hawthorne! Was it comedy or tragedy that you meant to write? Would you have us congratulate, or pity you on your "escape" from the rosy-cheeked Scotch lass? Did you lock yourself in your room and refuse nourishment for forty-eight hours? At all events you kept your pale Puritan humor in that gay galley of British fun.

The old English customs and manners of Yuletide,—the general atmosphere of festive preparation, the carolling of the "waits" on Christmas Eve, the service in the village church on Christmas Morn, the feasting in servants' hall and dining-room, the Yule-clog blazing on the broad hearth and the boar's head borne in with ceremony, the Wassail-Bowl and the Christmas-Pie, the songs and dances and games

CHRISTMAS GREENS

under the Lord of Misrule, the mummery in fancy dress, the ghost-stories by the fireside, the pervasive spirit of joviality and good comradeship between young and old, wise and simple, rich and poor,— these Christmas charms are nowhere set forth more enchantingly than in *The Sketch-Book* of Washington Irving. No wonder that Sir Walter Scott loved the book and the author. Yet even when he wrote, the genial Knickerbocker saw these ways and manners as antiquities, in a vanishing light; and he prefaced his essays with a quotation from a still earlier *Hue and Cry after Christmas:* "But is old, old, good old Christmas gone? Nothing but the hair of his good, gray, old head and beard left? Well, I will have that, seeing I cannot have more of him."

That seems to be the proper, regular, inevitable attitude to take about Christmas,—a kind of hail-and-farewell tone,—as if one would say, "let us have one more jolly good time, it may be the last." In that fruitful little book *Guesses at Truth*, written in 1827, I find this passage: "It was a practice worthy of our ancestors to fill their houses at Christmas time with their relations and friends; that when Nature was frozen and dreary out of doors, something might be found within doors 'to keep the pulses of their hearts in proper motion.' The custom, however, is only appropriate among people who happen to have hearts. It is bad taste to retain it in *these days*, when everybody worth hanging

"'*oublie sa mère
Et par bon ton se défend d'être père.*'"

So runs the song from age to age,—O good old times! O bad present times! O worse times to come!

I wonder what particular ways and manners of our own day the people of the twenty-second century will regard as especially picturesque and romantic.

There is plenty about Christmas in the treasure-house of English poetry, from Milton's glorious hymn to the lyrics of Eugene Field and Bliss Carman and Lady Lindsay. Richest and most Christmassy are the old ballads and carols and the poems by such writers as George Wither and Robert Herrick. But every poet when he comes to this subject shows something of his own personal character and sentiment,—his way of looking at life. Thus Stevenson writes a ballad of *Christmas at Sea*, and Kipling of *Christmas in India*.

CHRISTMAS GREENS

To some of us there is a peculiar brightness and sweetness in the memories associated with the homely household rites of putting up the greens and dressing the tree. This is done on Christmas Eve, after the younger children, or perhaps the grandchildren, have hung up their stockings and gone to bed. The elder children help. There is a joyous bustle and an air of secrecy about the business. If you hear a patter of small feet on the stair or see a tousled head peeping through the banisters, you must pretend to notice nothing.

The tall step-ladder must be brought up from the cellar, and it is usually very rickety. There are wreaths to be hung in windows and festoons to be looped over doors. A new way of decorating the pillars is much called for, but after many experiments you always come back to the old way. (Reader, I know not what your favorite way may be, but I am all for spirals of ground-pine.) Then the tree must be set up, on a white cloth, and decked with tiny candles, and hung with ornaments, old and new. (Don't forget the old ones, or the children will miss them.) Then the presents, the simpler the better, must be arranged in little piles under the tree.

CAMP-FIRES

Last of all, there are certain pictures,—"the old familiar faces," gone away, but never nearer than to-night—and each one of them must have its wreath of green, or perhaps a flower in a little vase before it. While you are doing this you have few words, but long, long thoughts.

Now it is midnight, and so to bed, for the children will have emptied their stockings by sunrise, and will be down in force to assault the room where the tree is locked in.

This is Christmas at home,—the best place. But who can tell where the holy day will find him,—how far away, how lonely, in what strange and hard surroundings? Shall he then be robbed of its joy? Shall it pass by without a bit of green and a blessing? Not if he have the heart to put forth his hand and touch the hem of its garment in passing.

Many a boy, in the years just passed, has had a rough Christmas. A letter came to me the other day from a young Canadian farmer, a stranger, who had been reading these Camp-fire papers, and this is what he wrote:

"The memory comes back embellished by many a pleasant and stirring adventure in the Balkans

CHRISTMAS GREENS

and takes one back to Christmas Day 1916. I was one of a British Artillery observation party and we were then leading a precarious existence on the bald, bare and lofty crown of Hill 380, which overlooked Ghergheli, that border town of many vicissitudes. Our attack, made a few days previously, had fizzled into chaos owing to small numbers and faulty liaison work with the Zouaves on our left. Incidentally our ration supply had failed for about five days and a brief, (very brief in fact,) survey of our larder found us with a leg of mutton of the 'white lean' (fat) description and three tins of the ubiquitous 'bully.' Of tea, sugar, bread or fuel there were none, and even if hope springs eternal according to Pope, it is apt to run rather in the valley of melancholy when a party of nine have to spend Christmas day in a poorly constructed shelter, and with a few pounds of raw meat as sole sustenance. The hilltop was exposed to machine-gun fire and also enfilade artillery *strafes*, and so movement of any kind was somewhat hazardous and even, in the circumstances, futile. I had joined the French *sous-lieutenant* in the O. P., and in saddened strains we conversed of *Noël* under more cheerful and homely conditions. Towards evening, observation became

CAMP-FIRES

difficult, and so, posting a lookout man in case of infantry flares for barrage, we crawled back to our inhospitable dugout and exchanged cigarettes with a view to await the possible, though highly improbable, arrival of the ration party. From the men's quarters came sounds of a melancholy dirge known to the troops as 'Looking for Rum.' A casual glance in the direction showed a faint trickle of light, wavering over the ground. My companion and I crawled from our sleeping-bags and crossed to the other dugout. It was a sight of great content to a pair of chilly and hungry mortals. In a battered tin helmet was a cheery fire, over which one of the telephonists fried bully beef in his dixie lid. Further inspection showed that the fire came from the outlaw leg of mutton! And so in its greasy and spluttering flame we saw, each in his own way, that life after all was worth living. We gathered round and sat in the warmth, nibbling at fried bully beef and swapping yarns, regardless of wars or War Lords. That Christmas night was well on its way to relegation among the happy and curious incidents of life, when a nasty shriek sounded and a dull 'phoof' of an exploding gas shell. We donned our gas helmets and in a spirit of braggadocio infused by our fire, allowed

CHRISTMAS GREENS

the mutton to burn on as a further inducement to the prowess of the Austrian gunners. Fortune must have felt benevolent, because we sat for about three quarters of an hour in the glow before it spluttered out. And the happy ending came at four in the morning with the ration train of mules.

> G. J. S.,
> Mankota, Sask., Canada."

Reader, do you think the war has spoiled Christmas? Do you believe the coming revolution, the social upheave, the triumph of materialism, the anarchy, or the dictatorship of the proletariat, or whatever may be before us, is going to destroy it, and leave no room for its return? I tell you, no!

Whatever turnings and overturnings, whatever calamity and ruin, are in store for this battered old world, you and I will never be poorer than the blessed Mary and Joseph when they walked to Bethlehem, and that same night

"The stars in the bright sky looked down where He lay,—
The little Lord Jesus asleep on the hay."

Whatever fantasies of government or no-government the brains of men may devise, the heart of

CAMP-FIRES

man will always ask and take a day of rest and peace, gladness and good-will to sweeten the long year.

So let us put up our bits of Christmas green, brother, with brave and cheerful hearts: and if we want something to strengthen and steady us, we will read by our camp-fire this verse of Charles Kingsley:

"O blessed day, which giv'st the eternal lie
  To self, and sense, and all the brute within;
O come to us amid this war of life;
To hall and hovel come: to all who toil,
In senate, shop, or study; and to those
Who sundered by the wastes of half a world,
Ill-warned and sorely tempted, ever face
Nature's brute powers, and men unmanned to brutes.
Come to them, blest and blessing, Christmas Day!
Tell them once more the tale of Bethlehem,
And kneeling shepherds, and the Babe Divine,
And keep them men indeed, fair Christmas Day."

XVII

ON SAYING GOOD-BYE

THE words consecrated by custom for use at meeting and at parting take on a certain formal quality by reason of their very sameness and oft repetition. For the most part they are but verbal gestures of politeness. We exchange them as mere tokens or counters of speech, without too curiously considering the metal whereof they are made, or their weight and value in the exact scales of reason.

On this ground some severe and haughty spirits affect to scorn them. Yet, after all, if they serve their purpose as signs of courtesy and friendliness in the quotidian come-and-go of life, why should we ask more of them? The greater, (though not the better,) part of our existence is composed of things whose general worth doth not depend upon their particular importance. They are of that "daily bread" which it behooves us to beseech with humility and accept with thankfulness. And believe me, reader, we digest it better without a careful computation of the calories which it contains, or a close count of the number of times we munch each morsel.

"Life is real, life is earnest," says the poet; and for that very reason, (being put together as we are of fatigable flesh and indefatigable spirit, in the proportion of a stack of fuel to a spark of flame,) our conduct of life should rightly have its large and fitting portion of things done easily and lightly, by routine, habit, and common consent.

Is the customary, the conventional, always to be despised? Shall a man always take the wrong side of the road only to prove himself original? After all the road hath but two sides, and he that taketh ever the wrong one, to show his liberal genius, is in the end as conventional a rogue as if he followed the harmless custom of the country. Nothing is more monotonous than a habitual irregularity.

I feel and admit the extraordinary attractions of change and novelty. No man can have more joy than I in a fresh adventure. Somewhat too much, indeed, of the experimental and venturesome there hath always been in my temperament, leading me often into situations from which it was difficult to emerge with credit and skin unbroken. Even now, many failures have not cured me of this fault.

ON SAYING GOOD-BYE

But familiarity also hath its charm, and I count it good that life is impregnated with it. The regular ways, the rules of the game, the customs of courtesy, and the common phrases of colloquial speech,— these are pleasant things in their season, (which is daily,) and without them our existence would be wayward, rude, exhausting, and far less tolerable than it is.

So with the salutations we exchange as we meet and part on the highway or the footpath of life: I find that a certain regularity and matter-of-course in them is not so much a defect, as a necessity, a wise and friendly concession to the limits of our inventive power. Meetings and partings are so common that their proper ritual must needs be of the commonplace. To make it otherwise would be to weave the plain family umbrella of cloth of gold.

What should we do if it were required of us to invent a new gesture of greeting every time we passed a lady of our acquaintance upon the street? Shall not the time-honored lifting of the hat suffice? You may give it a special flourish or grace-note, I admit, according to the beauty or dignity of the lady, or the degree of warmth in your regard for her. But these are matters of subtle shading and gradation. The gesture remains the same: "Madam, I take off my hat to you." It is the homage of the civilized man to the eternal womanly.

Granted, then, that our perpetual business of coming and going must evolve its formulas of *ave atque vale*, hail and farewell. Granted that we use them by convention and habit. Granted that we say "How do you do?" without waiting for an answer, and "Good day" without looking at the sky. What does it matter? 'Tis not the bare meaning of the word that counts, but the spirit in which it is spoken: good-will at meeting, good wishes at parting,—can you ask, or give, more?

Yet now and then something happens, inward or outward, to touch these familiar phrases with a finger-ray of light, so that we regard them more attentively, and reflect a while upon their origin and propriety. Maybe we would fain choose among the well-worn stock at our disposal that one greeting which hath most fitness to the moment and to our desire. Maybe we would fain lend to the mere syllables of farewell some special tone of kindness, comfort, or regret, to make it linger in the memory as a note of music in the air.

ON SAYING GOOD-BYE

Three things of this kind have moved me in the choice of a theme for this essay.

It is a word of parting from a year-long occupation, and from the friendly readers, near and far, who have sat with me in spirit beside these camp-fires.

Moreover, it belongs to the season of the year's decline and fall, that last of old December which must precede the first of new January; and though Charles Lamb calleth New Year's Day every man's second birthday, "the nativity of our common Adam," I note that his little essay on the subject, (true as his writing always is to the depth of human nature,) dwelleth more on the losses than on the gains of this anniversary. It is epicedial,—more of a farewell to the parting than a welcome to the coming guest,—and so is most poetry, ten times *vale*, to once *ave!*

Finally, I find myself now upon that stage of life's journey wherein the milestones, as Lowell said, seem altered into gravestones,—at least by the evening light. Or, if that figure is too sombre for you, (and I confess in my own judgment it hath too cemeterial a shade for a whole truth,) then let me use a simpler metaphor and say: I have come so far along the way that I have surely more partings to remember than meetings to expect, on the terrestrial road. So, then, it is thrice natural at this time that I should write a little essay "on saying good-bye."

The word has a beautiful, sacred meaning, which is lost to view when we spell it "Good-by." It is really a contraction of the phrase God-be-with-ye, and is even lovelier than the French "Adieu,"—a deep, holy word.

But I have often wondered why we have no parting phrase in English to express what we so clearly hear in other tongues,—the lively hope of meeting again. The Germans say *auf Wiedersehen*,—do you remember Lowell's lovely lyric with that title? —and the Italians, *a rivederci*, and the French, *au revoir*. All these are fitting and graceful words; they solace the daily separations of life with the pleasant promise that we shall see each other again, —*à bientôt*, the French say sometimes, as if to underline the wish that the next meeting may be soon.

Why should we be forced to use a foreign phrase for such a native feeling? Yet what English word is there that briefly and precisely utters this senti-

ON SAYING GOOD-BYE

ment? The nearest to it is the modern colloquialism, *So long!*

This comes, I fancy, from London; it is a bit of Cockney dialect. The dictionary of "Passing English of the Victorian Era," (suspicious title!) says that it is a corruption of the Jewish word *selah*, used in the Whitechapel district as a form of good-bye. Of this I have my doubts, both whether *selah* is used in that way, and whether it could be twisted into "so long." *Salaam*, or *shalōm*, the Eastern salutation of peace, seems to me a more likely derivation.

But why go so far afield? Have not the syllables *so long* in themselves a meaning, or at least a hint of meaning, that comes close to what we want? *So long* as we are parted may no harm befall you! Till we meet again, it will seem *so long!* I profess a liking for this child of the street who brings us what we need. I would take him in, adopt him, make him of the household. Has not his name been used already by Walt Whitman as the title of a good poem?

"While the pleasure is yet at the full, I whisper, *So long!*

. . . .

The unknown sphere, more real than I dreamed, more direct, awakening rays about me—*So long !*"

CAMP-FIRES

The next time I have to bid good-bye to a person not too dignified to be loved,—the next time I have to leave a scene or an edifice not too grandiose to be dear,—the next time, I am going to say, boldly and cheerfully, *So long!* and I care not who hears me.

It is a comfort that so many of our frequent partings in this sublunary sphere are temporary and carry with them the possibility of reunion. You shake hands regretfully with a good companion as you leave the ship,—you going east, he going west,—yet the world is small and round,—suddenly you and he turn a corner in Tokyo or Cairo, and there you are, gladly shaking hands again. You finish a task this year, and feel half lost as you let it go. But next year you shall find yourself busy with another task so like the first that you are sure it must be a reincarnation. You listen to some favorite actor or singer on a "farewell" tour, and sigh that you shall hear that voice no more. Yet it falls again upon your ear with the old, familiar cadence. I will not tell how many years ago I mourned at Mary Anderson's good-bye to the stage. But it is less than four years since I crept out of hospital in London and saw her again in *Pygmalion and Galatea*,

ON SAYING GOOD-BYE

her face and form as lovely, her liquid voice as entrancing as ever. Instead of "farewell" tours, let our well-beloved players give us "so long" tours, —with bright promise of return.

Of places, too, while we live there is ever this hope of another sight. I remember it was in the summer of 1888 that my lady Graygown and I bade farewell to Norway, not expecting to look upon those huge rounded mountains, green vales, and flashing waters again. Yet we saw them once more in the summer of 1916,—a most unlikely time,— the very heart and centre of the wild tempest of war. But the high hills of Voss gave back no echo of the world-tumult, and the swift-flowing Evanger had no tinge of crimson in its crystal current.

Peace rested round our little wooden cottage in its old-fashioned garden, on the point between the rushing river and the placid lake. Peace lay upon the far mountain-ridges, touched here and there with gleams of vanishing snow. Peace walked in the smooth, sloping meadows where the farmer-folk, prolonging pleasant labor late into the luminous night, hung the long racks of harvest with honey-scented hay. Peace floated in the air over the white rapids and translucent green pools of the stream where I cast the fly, and welcomed me walking home at midnight, carrying a brace of silver salmon, through the little square where the old villagers sat reading their newspapers by the lingering light of the northern sky and chatting

> "Of *new*, unhappy, far-off things
> And battles *yesterday*."

They gossiped also, I was sure, of homelier subjects,—

> "Familiar matter of to-day,—
> Some natural sorrow, loss, or pain,
> That has been, and may be again!"

Were they wrong, those ancient cronies, in taking their ease for an hour between ebbing daylight and rising dawn? And was I wrong to relish that peaceful fortnight of Norway revisited,—that steadying interval of quiet amid long months of strenuous duty on the very edge of war's black and bloody gulf? Nay then, if you blame me, reader, I must even bear your censure and contempt with the same philosophy which hath often helped me through life's hard places and bitter seasons.

Rough is the road, and often dark; frequented by outlaws and sturdy beggars; encumbered with

ON SAYING GOOD-BYE

wrecks of goodly equipages, and bodies of wounded travellers; full of cripples, and weary folk who are ready to faint and fall, and overladen beasts and men, and little lost children. At every turn we meet some disappointment or grief; in the long level stretches there is blinding heat and dust; and in the steep high places, cold and solitude. It is no primrose path, but a way of trial and trouble,—yes, at times a very *via dolorosa*, a way of grief.

And yet,—truth to tell,—are there not consolations and encouragements along the way? Resting-places like that house in Bethany where the Master found repose and love; wide and cheering outlooks from the brow of the hill, snug shelters in the bosom of the vale, camp-fires beneath the trees, wayside springs and fountains flowing among the rocks or trickling through the moss? Here will I stop, and stoop, and drink deep refreshment. Share with me! Music and friendship and nature,—sleep and dreams and rested waking in the light of morn,—to these we say not good-bye, but *so long!* They will always keep something for us, something to come back to; and if we are content with little, enough will be better than a feast.

Let us be honest with ourselves, and own that

the return is never quite the same as the first experience. It may be more, it may be less, but it always has a shade of difference. One thing is surely lost, the touch of surprise,—

> "The first fine careless rapture."

But by way of recompense there may come a deeper understanding, a more penetrating sympathy. It is so, I think, with great music. The third or fourth hearing of a noble symphony is perhaps the best. After that our delight varies, rising or falling with our mood, or with the outward circumstances. It is so with our best-beloved books, —companionable books,—books made for many readings. Their inward charm outwears their binding. As often as we revisit them after a brief separation they tell us something new, or something old with a new meaning. Yet one thing they offer us but once,—that which Keats describes in his sonnet "On First Looking into Chapman's Homer," —the joy of discovery. I confess that I would give a thousand dollars if I had never read *Henry Esmond* or *Lorna Doone*,—so that I might have the delight of reading them for the first time. But to make it quite complete perhaps I should need also to give

Camp-fires beneath the trees.

ON SAYING GOOD-BYE

an extra tip to the old Timekeeper and persuade him to set my clock back fifty years.

Many of our farewells are unconscious. You lend a book, and it is never brought back. You leave a place, and find no opportunity or pathway of return. You part from a friend, in anger or in sorrow, or it may be simply in the casual way with no special feeling,—and lo, the impenetrable curtain falls and the familiar face is hidden forever.

So much are we at the mercy of the unknown in this regard, that if we thought of it too closely and constantly it would unhinge reason and darken life with an intolerable gloom. Every departing carriage would bear black plumes, and on every ship that sailed away from us we should see a ghostly Charon on the bridge. We should be trying always to speak memorable "last words," instead of the cheerful, heartening *so long* which befits our ordinary occasions.

Here memory helps us to be sane, if we trust her. For we know that whatever hath entered deeply into our being is never altogether rapt away. The scene that we have loved,

"This town's fair face, yonder river's line,
  The mountain round it and the sky above,"

cannot be blotted from the inward vision. Nor can the soul that hath companioned ours through days and nights of bright and dark, turn a corner into oblivion. Though much is taken, more remains, —the very cadence of the voice, the clasp of the hand, the light in the eyes, "the sweet assurance of a look,"—these are treasures laid up in the heaven of remembrance where thieves do not break through nor steal.

Strange, how the last sight or the last word of a friend is not always the one that we recall most vividly. It is often some chance phrase, some unmeditated look or gesture. As if nature would say to us, (even as the Master said,) "Take no thought, be not anxious, for the morrow: be yourself to-day: so you will be remembered."

It hath been my lot, (having lived too long,) to conduct the funeral, or pronounce a memorial address, for many friends more renowned than I shall ever be,—Governor E. D. Morgan, ex-President Cleveland, Mark Twain, Clarence King, Edmund Clarence Stedman, John Bigelow, Hamilton Mabie, Sir William Osler, William Dean Howells,—and each of these lives in my memory by something very simple and not at all famous: a little name-

ON SAYING GOOD-BYE

less act of every-day kindness or courage, a self-revealing look of wonder or joy or regret, a good word let fall by hazard at the crossroads,—in brief a natural, unintended, real good-bye.

No doubt the world grows poorer by the loss of such friends,—yes, and of others most dear to my heart: the father whose firm loving hand set my fingers on life's bow and taught me to draw the arrow to the head; the bright-faced, daring lad on whom the half of my hope was staked; the girl with golden hair and warm brown eyes who was to me "a song in the house of my pilgrimage." Poorer, —*ay de mi!* What honest man dare deny that the parting from such comrades leaves life poorer? But against all inconsolable grievers and complainers, (and most of all against my own rebel thoughts,) I maintain and will ever maintain that life is also richer, immeasurably richer than it would be if these treasures had not been loaned to us for a while.

"Death," said Stevenson, "outdoes all other accidents because it is the last of them." There is something taken for granted in that word "accident" which I would not altogether admit. But when our grim and genial essayist goes on to speak of the slight influence which the prospect of death and its certain uncertainty exercise upon our daily conduct, and of the folly of allowing it to play the master in our thought and drive us like slaves to a hundred trembling compliances and evasions, I follow him fully and find him right.

A friend once begged Woodrow Wilson not to risk his life by marching in a long procession through an excited city,—"the country cannot afford to lose its President." Like a flash came his answer, "The country cannot afford to have a coward for President."

It is a strange fact, and worth noting, that those who have most to do with death,—like doctors and nurses and ministers,—are not much perturbed by it. They are of the same mind as Cato, in Cicero's dialogue *On Old Age:* "satisfy the call of duty and disregard death."

There is a curious illustration of this written by Procopius and cited by Anatole Le Braz in his wonderful book *La Légende de la Mort*. Here it is:

"At the beginning of the sixth century after Christ, the island of Britain was popularly believed to be the country of the dead. On the opposite coast of Brittany, says Procopius, there are scattered many villages whose peoples follow fishing

ON SAYING GOOD-BYE

and farming for their living. Subjects of the Franks in all other respects, they are excused from paying tribute, because of a certain service ('tis their word,) which they say has been laid upon them since a remote epoch: they claim to be under vows as 'the ferrymen of souls.' At night they are suddenly roused from sleep by a loud knocking at the door: a voice outside calls them to their task. They rise in haste; it would be vain to refuse obedience; a mysterious force drags them from their home to the beach. There they find boats, not their own, but stranger-boats. They look empty, but in reality they are full of people, loaded down almost to the sinking-point,—the water laps along the gunwale. The ferrymen embark and take the oars. An hour afterward, despite the heavy load of invisible passengers, they reach the island,—a voyage which ordinarily requires not less than a day and a night. Hardly have the boats touched shore when they are quickly lightened, though the rowers cannot see any of their fellow-travellers debark. A voice is heard on the land,—the same which waked the rowers in their beds. It is the Conductor of Souls presenting the dead whom he brings, one by one, to those appointed to receive them. The men he

CAMP-FIRES

calls by their fathers' names; the women, if there are any, by the names of their husbands; and of each shade he tells what work it did while living."

There the legend breaks off. But what becomes of the boats? And what of the ferrymen of souls, with their oars dripping, and their tanned faces gleaming in the misty starlight? Undoubtedly they row home to their Breton coast, and go to bed and sleep late, and rise again to their fishing and their farming, and day after day are busy and lazy and quarrelsome and tranquil and merry and unsatisfied, (even as you and I,) until the next knocking at the door by night, and the next call from the dark, and the time, at last, when their own names will be on the list of passengers.

For what port? Methinks I know; for One who is worthy of all trust, my Pilot, hath spoken a name to me and told me not to be afraid. But where it lies, that haven of salvaged ships and of forgiven failures, and when or on what course it will be approached, I know not, friend, any more than you.

The guide-posts of the sea are the stars. And all its mighty waters lie in the hollow of an almighty hand.

So good-bye, reader,—a good voyage,—so long!

FELLOW TRAVELLERS
MEMORIÆ POSITA

XVIII

AN OLD-STYLE AMERICAN*

THE long, useful, honorable career of John Bigelow was marked from beginning to end by a joyful attention to human duties. He was a human fountain of sanely directed energy. He loved to be in the thick of things. He was never willing to retire, like Shelley's imaginary reformers, into a cave. He steadfastly pursued the active life.

But, at the same time, he was a follower of the contemplative life. He loved truth, and sought for the Heavenly Wisdom more than for hid treasure. Finding her, his heart was glad, and he took counsel with her in the night season. Life was intensely real to him, and intensely interesting, because it meant more than the eye can see or the ear can hear. Guided by the Bible, and by Swedenborg, and by such poets as Milton and Wordsworth and Bryant, he learned to read the inward heart of things beneath their outward form. But the more his

*Read before the Century Club, New York, March 9, 1912.

meditation deepened, the more his action was invigorated and directed to useful ends.

He was in fact a common-sense mystic, refusing to let life be divided, or to content himself with either half. He belonged to the double tribe of Joseph, both dreamers and doers, men of the type of Milton and Lincoln and Pasteur, who are better citizens on earth because they hold fast to their citizenship in Heaven.

John Bigelow was born in 1817, at the village which is now called Malden, on the shores of the Hudson River, between Kingston and Catskill. The love of that noble stream ran through his life; beside it he built his country residence, "The Squirrels"; and one of his latest public utterances was a fervid, almost fiery, letter to the people, in connection with the Hudson-Fulton Celebration in 1909, urging that the only fitting way to honor the memory of those men would be to protect the waters of their river from pollution and its banks from desecration, that it might flow brightly and bravely to the sea, "ready to appease the hunger and thirst of millions." There was always something concrete and practical in the idealism of John Bigelow.

AN OLD-STYLE AMERICAN

The same homely, concrete quality marks the boyhood chapter in his "Retrospections of an Active Life." He makes you see his birthplace, the old farmhouse, lighted by tallow dips, warmed by huge wood-fires, with its big kitchen, its spinning-wheels and tubs of goldenrod dye, its cask of soft soap in the woodshed, and its cellar crammed with all sorts of provisions, "the very stomach of the house." He takes you with him driving the cows to pasture, and into the snake-haunted Eden of a certain strawberry-meadow (where he was duly punished for picking fruit on Sunday) and over the river to a dull school at Sharon, and back again to his native district school, which he says was "the only school in which I was conscious of having received any thorough or conscientious instruction from my teachers." He gives you a glimpse of a spelling-bee, a country circus, the disastrous consequences of his first cigar, his first attempt to commend himself to a little girl by wearing his Sunday clothes on a week-day. He shows you his father's big country store by the river, and the sloops that carried its multifarious trade, and the father himself, six feet four of rugged manhood, a Bible Christian and a convinced Presbyterian, but withal a good provider, a careful farmer and shrewd trader, "not ascetical, but always cheerful and sensible," a very human sort of Puritan and good to live with.

Such homes as this were favorable starting-places for young Americans. They had enough roughness to be bracing, enough restraint to be sobering, enough elevation of thought and talk to be ennobling, and enough liberty to quicken the heart with the joy of living.

Young Bigelow spent three years at a college in Hartford without getting much good, and finished his course at Union College without getting any harm. In his eighteenth year, he left home to study law; starting with a firm at Hudson, where he used to sweep out the office before breakfast; and then going to New York, where he began making those friendships of the royal kind which are only possible to one who has himself a royal spirit,—among which the first place must be given to his intimacies with William Cullen Bryant, Charles O'Conor, and Samuel J. Tilden. After that, comes the long list of men who were brought into relation with him by a common interest in public affairs,—Sumner, Preston King, Seward, E. D. Morgan, Cobden, John Bright, William Hargreaves, Laboulaye, Mon-

AN OLD-STYLE AMERICAN

talembert,—it would be impossible to name them all. No man was ever richer in the fruits of human intercourse than John Bigelow, for in this kind he was both a generous giver and a grateful receiver.

Plutarch tells us that Plato, at the close of his life, found cause for thankfulness in three things: that he was born a man, not a beast; that he was born a Greek, not a barbarian; and that he was born a contemporary of Sophocles. John Bigelow was one of Plutarch's men, and I think he would have put his reasons for thanksgiving thus: "that I was born a man; that I was born an American; that I was born a contemporary of Bryant." For the character and genius of this illustrious friend he cherished the most sincere reverence. He tells us that, long after their daily intercourse was terminated, it was his custom to test what he had done, or proposed to do, by asking himself: "How would Mr. Bryant act under similar circumstances?" "I rarely applied this test," he adds, "without receiving a clear and satisfactory answer."

Such a talent for friendship as this is one of the marks of excellence, not of the Napoleonic type, but of the human, companionable, serviceable kind.

CAMP-FIRES

Admitted to the bar in 1838, he made respectable, but not rapid, progress in his profession, helping to make both ends meet by teaching and by writing literary articles for the reviews and political articles for the newspapers. His first public appointment was as an inspector of the State Prison at Sing Sing, in which position he did good work for reform.

In 1846 the alleged war with Mexico inaugurated the real conflict between Slavery and Freedom. Mr. Bigelow took his part with that section of the Democracy known as the Free-Soil Party, of which Martin Van Buren, Silas Wright, and Samuel J. Tilden were leaders. Mr. Bigelow's force as a writer increased as his interest in national affairs grew more intense. In 1848 he was invited to join Mr. Bryant in the ownership and editing of the *Evening Post*, the ablest organ of the Free-Soil Democracy. Charles O'Conor, although belonging to the other wing of the party, generously indorsed the notes which were necessary to finance the arrangement. Thus Mr. Bigelow entered upon the most active and strenuous period of his labors, and worked as a fighting editor from 1848 till 1861, when he sold his interest in the paper and resigned his chair to his friend Mr. Parke Godwin.

AN OLD-STYLE AMERICAN

Of the policy of the *Post* during those years we have his own description. "The questions we had to discuss, happily for me, were mainly moral questions. We were for freedom against slavery, which was the *pièce de résistance* from year in to year out. We were the leading, if not the only, champion of a revenue tariff as against a protective tariff, in all the Northern States. We hunted with almost reckless audacity every base or selfish influence that was brought to bear either upon legislation or administration. Hence, although we always professed to be Democrats and to preach what we regarded as the genuine principles of popular sovereignty, we were never regarded as part of the machine, and rarely were even as tolerant of it as perhaps at times we might well have been."

Precisely so. Not only toward "the machine" but toward other objects and adversaries, Mr. Bigelow's early and middle manner sometimes betrayed a lack of tolerance that bordered on acerbity. He was not an easy-going man, nor by nature soft-spoken. His disposition was sanguine; his temper a distinct conductor of ardent heat; his will strong to the point of obstinacy. Doubtless the temptations of an editor's irresponsible power, of which he wrote so feelingly in his "Life of Bryant," may have led him into some of those *errata* that he deplored as inseparable from the conduct of frail and ignorant humanity. But all this only makes it the more remarkable and praiseworthy that his later manner should be so marked by consideration and urbanity, that he became to us in the Century Club the very type and model of the high courtesy which (by way of sad confession) we call "old-fashioned."

A gentleman, I take it, is one who is not incapable of anger, but capable of learning to control it, and who, for reasons of good-will, sets his intelligence to avoid equally the giving and the taking of offense.

But the years preceding the Civil War were hot times, in which offense abounded. Through all that heat and turbulence and confusion, the *Evening Post* held steadily, if not always serenely, to its moral principles, and rendered great service in inspiring and guiding the independent Democrats, whose courage and self-sacrificing loyalty made possible the foundation of the Republican party, the election of Abraham Lincoln, and the preservation of the Union.

Before leaving this part of my subject, I must say a word as to the kind of Democracy in which

AN OLD-STYLE AMERICAN

Mr. Bigelow believed, and to which he remained faithful throughout his life. He was no friend to absolutism in popular sovereignty any more than in monarchy or empire. He held that the rule of the people should be self-limited and self-directed by constitutional restraint; that the use of the suffrage should be for the choice of representative and executive officers, and for such amendment of the Constitution as becomes necessary from time to time; that the object of the Republic is to safeguard the development of the native energies of its citizens unfettered by superfluous legislation; and above all that a democracy, while it may defend itself by arms, can only propagate its ideas by example. He was in fact *a collective individualist*.

He thought, not that the Old is better than the New, but that the Old is necessary to the New, its root and spring. Progressivism he disliked for its reactionary tendencies. He expected no more from political organizations and combinations than was in them, knowing that "governments like clocks would run down as they were wound up." He was of the school of Solon, who tried "so to frame his laws as to make it evident to the Athenians that it would be more for their interest to observe them than to transgress them." He belonged to the party of the wise men in all the ages,—the party that knows the only sure way to better the social fabric is to improve the moral fibre out of which it must be woven.

It was during his journalistic period that three great good fortunes came to Mr. Bigelow; first, the beginning of his happy domestic life, by his marriage with Miss Jane Poultney in 1850; second, the commencement of his life as an author in 1852, with a volume called "Jamaica in 1850; or the Effect of Fifty Years of Freedom on a Slave Colony"; third, the recovery of his faith in the Bible, through an acquaintance in 1853 with the works of Emanuel Swedenborg. So, close together, he found the three immediate jewels of the soul: companionship, vocation, illumination.

In August, 1861, President Lincoln appointed him to the American Consulship in Paris, with the idea that he should give special attention to the Press in France, and to the formation of public opinion favorable to the United States. A man better qualified by nature and training for such a task could not have been discovered.

Mr. Bigelow was a representative of the Spirit

AN OLD-STYLE AMERICAN

of America in the sense that he gave a personal impression of the qualities that created the Revolution and the Republic: self-reliance, fair play, energy, love of the common order, and desire of individual development. These he embodied with a singular charm of simplicity and dignity in France during our Civil War, even as Benjamin Franklin had embodied them with a like charm during our Revolution.

The services of these two persons of native distinction and shrewdness,—the one in winning the alliance of France in our struggle for liberty; the other in preventing the hostility and interference of France in our struggle for Union,—were of a value so inestimable that it is difficult to measure between them. If Bigelow's task was easier than Franklin's by reason of the greater national resources and powers which supported it, at the same time it was more difficult by just so much as the character of Louis XVI was more sincere, generous, and noble than the character of Napoleon III. It was a fascinating turn of fortune that Bigelow was able, at the close of his French residence, to recover for his country the manuscript of *Franklin's Autobiography*, and to publish the *editio princeps* of the correct text of that extraordinary little book, the first American classic.

In 1865 he was appointed by Lincoln to succeed the late W. L. Dayton as Envoy Extraordinary and Minister Plenipotentiary to the Court of France, in which office President Johnson continued him until Bigelow's resignation in 1866. His work in connection with the French occupation of Mexico and the preposterous but none the less dangerous schemes involved in what he called "The Chromo Empire" of Maximilian, was done with a firm, delicate, and masterly hand.

He conveyed warnings to Napoleon and his rather sky-rockety ministers without making threats. He encouraged the government at Washington to wait with dignity for the inevitable *débâcle* of the Franco-Austrian house-of-cards, rather than to plunge rashly into a superfluous war in Mexico.

His letters and sayings of this period are full of pithy eloquence and homespun wit. For instance, he says to Napoleon's Foreign Minister, "It is as idle to suppose that you can disregard a great national feeling as that you can annihilate a particle of matter." To R. H. Dana he writes, "I hope

AN OLD-STYLE AMERICAN

you will do what you can to prevent the country getting into a false position about Mexico and converting a sentiment into a policy." To Seward: "There is a way of saying that you won't be bullied that amounts to bullying." Of a certain bishop: "He is one of those who are for all the freedoms when they serve the Church and against them when they don't." Of President Johnson beginning his conflict with Congress: "I wish he had found means to plough around this stump instead of running smack into it." Of the approach of the Austro-Prussian War: "Europe is going to war as people sometimes go to the brandy-bottle to get rid of their own domestic troubles, and with a prospect of the same success."

Still more clearly do Mr. Bigelow's natural sagacity and power of just estimation come out in his appreciation of President Lincoln. "The greatness of Lincoln must be sought for in the constituents of his moral nature. I do not know that history has made a record of the attainment of any corresponding eminence by any other man who so habitually, so constitutionally, did to others as he would have them do to him. He was not a learned man. But the spiritual side of his nature was so highly organized that it rendered superfluous much of the experience which to most men is indispensable,—the choicest prerogative of genius. In the ordinary sense of the word, Lincoln was not a statesman. The issues presented to the people at the Presidential election of 1860 were, to a larger extent, moral questions, humanly speaking, than were those presented at any other Presidential election. . . . Looking back upon the Administration, and upon all the blunders which from a worldly point of view, Lincoln and his advisers seemed to have made, and then pausing to consider the results of that Administration, . . . we realize that we had what above all things we most needed, a President who walked by faith and not by sight; who did not rely upon his own compass, but followed a cloud by day and a fire by night, which he had learned to trust implicitly."

After Mr. Bigelow's return to America, he was appointed by his friend Governor Tilden, in 1875, as a member of the Commission which broke up the dishonest Canal Ring of New York. In the same year he was elected Secretary of State. With these

AN OLD-STYLE AMERICAN

two exceptions, his life from 1867 to 1911 was withdrawn from political office and devoted to public service.

Mature at sixty, mellow at seventy, vigorous at eighty, venerable at ninety, he followed and finished his chosen course of usefulness, with eye undimmed, joy unabated, and courage undismayed.

To those of us who knew and loved him in his later years, he seemed a living link between the present and the past. But his power to join old times with ours lay not only in his longevity, but also in his vitality. His interest in the present days was no less than in the days that are gone. He joyfully admitted that many changes in the world had been for the better.

He was not one of those old men who think to show their greatness by making others feel small, their venerableness by making others feel juvenile. Retired from business and politics, he did not live in retirement and idleness, but in the open, willingly assuming such labors, burdens, and studies as he conceived would enable him to employ his undiminished strength *gratis* for the benefit of his country and his city.

CAMP-FIRES

Remembering this beautiful and fruitful period of John Bigelow's autumn, we think not so much of the length of his life as of its nobility, and recall for him the words of that fine inscription in the Latin Chapel of Christ Church, Oxford:

"Non enim quae longaeva est senectus honorata est, neque numero annorum multorum; sed prudentia hominibus est canities, et vita immaculata est senilis aetas."

His literary works were considerable, both in number and importance; and in all of them that I have read, the substance and the style are marked and distinguished by the personality of the author. This is one of the indispensable qualities of Literature, which calls no children legitimate who do not resemble their father.

Chief among his books, I would name his *Life of Samuel J. Tilden;* his admirable monograph on *William Cullen Bryant*, whom he always regarded as "America's greatest poet"; his profoundly interesting and spiritually suggestive volume on *The Mystery of Sleep;* and finally his three rich tomes of *Retrospections of an Active Life,*—a title which he emphasized with some

AN OLD-STYLE AMERICAN

particularity, and rightly, for it defined his purpose and revealed his character.

There was always something definite and decided about John Bigelow. He knew what he thought, and said it. His courtesy was not of the nature of compromise, but of the respect due to others and to himself. In his opinions, his theories of life, even his personal tastes, he was clear and positive. His preferences for the teachings of Swedenborg, for the practice of homeopathy, for the doctrine of free trade, and for temperance, fresh air, and cheerfulness as the elements of a sound hygiene, were subject to polite discussion but not liable to change. I imagine that nothing short of an amendment to the Constitution would have induced him to give up his horses for an automobile.

It is pleasant and profitable to bring to mind his rugged face, his lofty figure, his simple-stately ways as he moved among us, bearing the burden of his ninety years with a certain half-humorous, half-pathetic, wholly virile grace. Recall his presence as he presided in the Century library, cheerfully upholding the tradition of the fellowship from which all of his contemporaries and most of his earlier friends had vanished. Recollect him as he

CAMP-FIRES

appeared fifteen months ago, at the meeting of the American Academy in the New Theatre, to read his audaciously delightful paper on "A Breakfast with Alexander Dumas," or six months later when he spoke at the opening of the Public Library. Or best of all, remember him as he used to receive his friends last fall, in his sunny book-room at 21 Gramercy Park, sitting in his high-backed chair, reading, dreaming, or working, surrounded by the loving care of children and grandchildren.

Always where he could put his hand upon them, a copy of the Bible and a volume of Swedenborg lay beside him. Always he was ready to talk with unfailing interest and vividness of old times or new times, of the progress of the city, of the union of the churches on the basis of their main and real beliefs, of the improvement of the world, or of the mysteries of Heaven.

Thus he waited, not idly but busily, not fearfully but bravely, "in the confidence of a certain faith, in the comfort of a reasonable, religious and holy hope," for the coming of the great change, the great liberation, the great promotion from an active life to a redeemed immortality of ser-

AN OLD-STYLE AMERICAN

vice. So John Bigelow passed away on December 19, 1911:

> "His twelve long sunny hours
> Bright to the edge of darkness: then the calm
> Repose of twilight and a crown of stars!"

XIX

INTERPRETER'S HOUSE*

A TRIBUTE to the memory of Hamilton Wright Mabie must be full of deep and warm affection if it would express in any measure the thoughts and feelings of the many who knew him personally in the crowded pilgrimage of American life.

He was a man with a genius for friendship. Religious by nature and holding to Christian faith and ideals with unalterable conviction, he had a simple, beautiful, reasonable quality of manhood which kept him from ever becoming a bigot, a fanatic, or a sentimentalist. He understood human nature, with all its faults and twists, and he loved it notwithstanding all. Steering his own course with a steady hand, he wished not to judge or dominate other men, but only to help them to see the star by which he steered and to make its light more useful to them for guidance. Those who came to him for counsel got it clean and

* Read before the American Academy of Arts and Letters, April 10, 1919.

INTERPRETER'S HOUSE

straight, often with that touch of humor which was the salt of his discourse. Those who disliked and scorned him as an "old fogy," and pursued him with a strange malice of petty mockery, found him silent, tolerant, content to go forward with his own work, and ready to help them if they got into trouble. He was the most open-minded and kind-hearted of men. To his acquaintances and his thousands of auditors on his lecture tours, he was a voice of tranquil wisdom, genial wit, and serene inspiration. To his intimates he was an incomparable comrade.

I came to know him well only after he had passed middle life. But I felt sure that the spirit which was in him then, had animated him from the beginning, and I know that it continued to illuminate him to the end. Mabie was not a man to falter or recant. He advanced. He fulfilled the aim of Wordsworth's "Happy Warrior," who

>"when brought
>Among the tasks of real life hath wrought
>Upon the task that pleased his childish thought."

He was born at Cold Spring, New York, in 1846, and graduated from Williams College in 1867, and

CAMP-FIRES

from the Columbia College Law School in 1869. But the practice of law as a profession did not attract or suit him. In 1879 he became an editorial writer for *The Christian Union*, a religious periodical of broadening scope and influence, which developed under the leadership of Lyman Abbott and Hamilton Mabie and an able staff into the liberal, national, Christian weekly well named *The Outlook*.

Mabie's work on this paper was constant, devoted, happy, and full of quiet stimulus to clearer thinking and better living. Most of his articles, which must have numbered thousands during his service of thirty-seven years, were unsigned. But they bore the image and superscription of his fine intelligence, broad sympathies, and high standards both in literature and in life. They were not sermons. They were plain words of wisdom uttered in season. They were sometimes pungent,—for he had a vivid sense of righteousness,—but they were never malicious or strident. They were the counsels of a well-wisher. He hated evil, but when he struck at it he desired to help those whom it had deluded and enslaved. For the most part he wrote from the positive rather than from the negative

INTERPRETER'S HOUSE

side, preferring the praise of right to the condemnation of wrong. Something in his character permeated his style. A certain unpretending reasonableness, a tranquil assurance of the ultimate victory of light over darkness, an understanding sense of the perplexities and shadows which overcast our mortal life, gave to the words which he wrote from week to week a power of penetration and persuasion. They entered myriads of homes and hearts for good. In this service to modern life through the editorial pages of *The Outlook* he continued gladly and faithfully until he died, on New Year's Eve, 1916.

During this long period of professional labor as a writer for the press, he developed a national influence perhaps even wider as a public lecturer and an author.

No man in America was more welcome to an intelligent audience, for a lyceum lecture or a commencement address, than Hamilton Mabie. Here his personal qualities had full play, even more than in his writing. His radiant nature, his keen sense of humor, his ready and attractive manner of speech, his sympathy with all sorts and conditions of men and women, gave him quick and easy access to his listeners. He reached them because he took the trouble to open the doors.

The material of his lectures, as in the case of Emerson, was that which he afterward used in his books. But when he was speaking it was put in a different form,—more free, more colloquial, adapted to the occasion. Why should a speaker regard his auditors as cast-iron receptacles for a dose of doctrine? Mabie never did that. But he always had something to say that was serious, well-considered, worth thinking about. That was the reason why thoughtful people liked to hear him. He was a popular lecturer in the best sense of the phrase.

The demands upon his time and strength in this field were incessant. In addition he met the constant appeal of humane and hopeful causes looking to the betterment of social life,—like the Kindergarten Society of which he was for many years the president. To these calls he was always ready to respond. It was his self-forgetfulness in such work that exhausted his strength and brought on his final illness. He was a soldier on the firing-line of human progress. In that cause he was glad to give his life.

His books have deserved and had a wide reading.

They show the clear carefulness of this thinking, the depth of his love for nature and human nature, his skill as a writer of translucent English.

Nothing could be better for the purpose for which they were intended than the volumes in which he rendered, for the boys and girls of to-day, the great stories and legends of the past,—*Norse Stories from the Eddas, Myths Every Child Should Know, Heroes Every Child Should Know*, and so on.

But much more significant and original is the series of books in which he made his contribution to the art of essay-writing,—*My Study Fire, Under the Trees and Elsewhere, Short Studies in Literature.* These are rich in the fruits of observation in the home, the library, the great out-of-doors,—

> "The harvest of a quiet eye
> That broods and sleeps on his own heart."

These volumes were followed by others in which he expressed his deepening thoughts on the unity and the beauty of life in brief essays on *Nature and Culture, Books and Culture, Work and Culture, The Life of the Spirit,* and *The Great Word,*—by which he means *Love*, not blind and selfish, but open-eyed, intelligent, generous. A fine ideal guides the course of all these essays,—an ideal of the co-operation of nature and books and work in the unfolding of personality. Culture, in that sense, was Mabie's conception of the best reward that life has to give. *Kultur*, in the German sense, machine-made and iron-bound, he despised and hated. For this and other reasons he was ardent for the cause of the free and civilized nations against Germany in the barbaric war which she forced upon the world in 1914.

But the bulk of his work was done before this sharp and bitter crisis, in a period of general tranquillity, through which his writing flows like a pure and fertilizing stream in a landscape. He was an optimist, but not of the rose-water variety. He knew that life involves painful effort, hard conflict. Nevertheless, he believed that for those who will face the conflict and make the effort, help and victory are sure. He was a critic, delighting to read and comment upon the great books,—Homer, the Greek Tragedies, the Mediæval Epics, Dante, Shakespeare, Milton, and the more modern classics. But he was not a technical and scholastic critic. He sought to catch the spirit and meaning of the literature which he loved. His work always re-

INTERPRETER'S HOUSE

minds me of that passage in the *Pilgrim's Progress* which describes the "House of the Interpreter." The beauty of his comment on the classics is that it has a way of being right about their real significance.

This is true of his most important critical work, —*William Shakespeare, Poet, Dramatist, and Man*. On this volume he spent long, loving, patient study and toil. The result was one of the best, clearest, most readable and illuminating books in Shakespearean literature. Its central thesis,—that Shakespeare's *poetic* genius, his gift of vision, passion, and imagination, was the spring of his power, and that therefore, despite our imperfect knowledge of his biography, we may be sure of his greatness as a man,—is thoroughly sound. It is set forth with admirable lucidity and abundant illustration.

There is one of Mabie's books which is less known than others. It is called *A Child of Nature*. It represents his first and only attempt, so far as I know, in the field of fiction. But it is fiction of a peculiar type,—no plot, little dialogue, no incidents except birth and death and the ordinary run of life in the New England village where "John Foster" spent his days. The theme of the book, developed with deep fidelity and subtle beauty, is the growth of this quiet, simple, lonely man in fellowship with nature and a few great books. He dies silent and alone, never having learned to speak out to the world, or even to his neighbors, the wisdom which he has garnered. But some brief daily record of his experiences, his thoughts, the light of life that has come to him, he has written down and leaves behind him. Then comes a young man of another type, Ralph Parkman, scholar, traveller, and author, to live in the old farmhouse. He finds the forgotten papers, and their sincerity and beauty take hold of him. He gives them the form and finish which they need, and sends them out to the world.

"It was a little book which finally went forth from the old house, but it was very deep and beautiful; like a quiet mountain pool, it was far from the dust and tumult of the highways, and there were images of stars in it. With the generosity of a fine spirit the younger man interpreted the life of the older man through the rich atmosphere of his own temperament, but there was nothing in the beautiful flowering and fruitage which the world received from his hand which was not potentially

INTERPRETER'S HOUSE

in the heart and mind of John Foster. The silent man had come to his own; for God had given him a voice. After the long silence of a lifetime he spoke in tones which vibrated and penetrated, not like great bells swung in unison in some high tower, but like dear familiar bells set in old sacred places, whose sweet notes are half-audible music and half-inaudible faith and prayer and worship."

With these words of his own I leave this brief, imperfect tribute to Hamilton Mabie as man and author. The value of his work is still living in the hearts of his hearers and readers whom it has enlightened and encouraged. It is worthy to be treasured. To me the memory of his friendship means more than words can tell.

XX

THE HEALING GIFT*

To divide and distinguish a man from the profession in which he is engaged,—to make the measure of his success depend merely on his technical proficiency and reckon his fame only by the discoveries and inventions which he has made,—seems to me foolish. There may be some professions in which this is possible; for example, engineering, where one has to deal chiefly with the tenacity of certain minerals; or astronomy, where one observes the motions and calculates the constitution of distant stars; or chemistry, in which the supposed elements of imagined matter are tested by experiment and recombined by hypothesis. But in the more personal professions, such as teaching and medicine, where the unexplained mystery of our human nature is part of the material to be dealt with, no professor can be truly excellent or memorable unless he has within him the qualities which

*Read at Johns Hopkins University, Baltimore, March 22, 1920.

THE HEALING GIFT

belong to the make-up of a really great man. Such a man was Sir William Osler, world-renowned physician.

Of his achievements in medicine and surgery, Doctor Welch and other honored colleagues have written and spoken with authority which is indisputable. I speak only of the personality in the profession, the man William Osler, who was a famous doctor, and had the healing gift.

It was in Baltimore that I first met him, when he was Professor of Medicine at Johns Hopkins University. He had behind his name a score of degrees and decorations from various universities all over the world,—honors fairly won by his work. But this was not the main thing about the man. He bore his honors, to use the American phrase, "not so that you would notice it." He was like the friend whom Tennyson describes in *In Memoriam:*

> "wearing all that weight
> Of learning lightly like a flower."

He was the simplest, most modest, and most charming of the companions whom I met at the hospitable dinner-tables of Baltimore.

Do you remember his topaz eyes, never inquisitive but always searching and comprehending; his mouth with no set smile fixed on it, but always quick to respond in sympathy; the tranquil, friendly, understanding expression of his beautiful, dark, oval face?

I was never fortunate enough to be his patient, but I could have trusted him to "the crack o' doom." I should have felt that he would do for me all that man can do.

Two friends of mine I ventured to commend to his care in England. One was a poor governess. The other was an English official of high rank. To both of them he gave an equal care and interest. Both of them are living now, but, alas, the friend who helped them through their hard time is gone.

The next time that I saw Doctor Osler intimately was in Paris, in the winter of 1908–1909. As always, the meeting with him was delightful. But far more illuminative and instructive were the reports that came from my son, who was then a scholar at Magdalen College in Oxford. He wrote me that Sir William and Lady Osler were like father and mother to the American students there.

At an evening party, Doctor Osler would put his hand on the shoulder of a shy boy and say: "You

THE HEALING GIFT

don't care for dancing. Come into the library with me." And then he would show the boy wonderful treasures among the old books.

The last thing that Doctor Osler gave me was his monograph on the bookworm,—*anobium paniceum*—against which he had a justifiable human hatred, but which, none the less, he was careful to study scientifically and to depict accurately in a fine plate of which he was proud. His attitude toward this noxious beast was very much like that which he held toward the Prussian *Kultur*, and other deadly microbes.

Looking through his writings I find a thousand things which interest me. His most characteristic volume *Æquanimitas* recommends that steady tranquillity of demeanor which is essential to the practical work of a physician; but underneath that counsel I find the distinctly Christian words of patience, charity, and hopefulness. I should like to add to the title of the book, "Magnanimitas."

In an address which he delivered to the medical students at Toronto, he said the "Master Word of Medicine" is Work. From this he went on to teach the three great lessons of life. "First, learn to consume your own smoke. Second, we are not here to get all we can for ourselves, but to make the lives of others happier. (This he supports by the authority of Christ.) Third, the law of the higher life is only fulfilled by love, *i. e.*, charity."

His writings and addresses are saturated with the Bible. But he quotes also from other sources.

In one brief address, called *Man's Redemption of Man*, made to the students of Edinburgh in 1910, I have noted the following quotations and references: Isaiah, Christ, Confucius, Cardinal Newman, Euripides, Edwin Markham, Deuteronomy, John Bunyan, Sir Thomas Browne, Sir Henry Maine, Plato, Sir Gilbert Murray, Robert Browning, Pythagoras, Hippocrates, Galen, Copernicus, Charles Darwin, Aristotle, Galileo, Milton, Stevenson, Rudyard Kipling, Weir Mitchell, Poe, Prodicus, and Shelley,—with whose verse the address closes. Quotation on this scale would swamp an ordinary man. But Osler was not an ordinary man. He was a true scholar, who read much and assimilated all that he read.

The breadth of his knowledge was an inspiration to his practice as a physician. It was not only medicine that he understood, but life. He gave his patients confidence and serenity, and thereby

THE HEALING GIFT

helped them to get the benefit of such other medicines as he prescribed.

In nothing was he an extremist: certainly not a pessimist; hardly an optimist, because he knew too much; distinctly a meliorist, because he believed that the advance of medical science would bring great good to mankind. Yet I am sure he felt that life meant more than mere living on earth. This, I think, is the conclusion of his lectures on *Science and Immortality* delivered at Harvard University in 1904.

The last time that I saw him, gracious and vital as ever, was in Oxford in the spring of 1917, when America had just awakened after long slumber, and taken her right place in the World War. Osler's only child, Revere, was on the front-line, fighting for justice and freedom. That was where his father and mother wanted him to be. Anxiety for their boy, so young, so bright, so rare and delicate in promise, was in their hearts day and night. Yet it only made them kinder, more thoughtful and generous in ministering to others.

I had just come out of hospital in London after slow recovery from a slight injury received in the trenches at Verdun. Doctor Osler had known of it and had sent me wise counsel and help. Now he took me with him through the wonderful war-hospitals of Oxford, knowing that it would humble and strengthen my heart to see the men who were bearing and suffering a thousandfold more than I, for the good cause. As we passed through the long wards of the Schools Building, and among the tents where the outdoor patients were sheltered in the lovely New College Gardens, faces brightened, eyes lit up with affection and hope in the presence of the beloved physician. There was something healing, calming, stimulating in the soul of the man, shining through his outward form. He pretended nothing. He knew all that there was to be known. He never faltered nor flinched from the facts. His keen and evident sensibility never interfered with his steadiness of hand or coolness of nerve. His very look seemed to say, "Be brave, be patient, remember the other fellows, do your best to get well and I will help you; for the rest we must all put our trust in God."

Osler's sense of humor was native, unconquerable, and always full of human sympathy. He upheld and illustrated the ancient Hippocratic standards in the practice of medicine: "learning, sa-

THE HEALING GIFT

gacity, humanity, probity." No one could have laughed more heartily than he at the refutation which his own life gave to his jocose confession, in his farewell address at Johns Hopkins in 1905, of two "harmless obsessions," namely, that men above forty are comparatively useless, and men above sixty are cumberers of the ground. This was a jest so fine that the so-called "reading-public" in America could not possibly understand it. Nor could they be expected to note that the suggestion in regard to the use of chloroform to get rid of people over sixty was a quotation from Anthony Trollope, to which Osler distinctly declined to give his approval, because as he said, "my own time is getting so short."

Yet, after all, it was not so very short: fourteen years were left to him, and he filled them to the brim with noble work and happy play. Never was he more alive, more useful, more helpful and healing to his fellow men than in those years,

"Serene and bright,
And lovely as a Lapland night,"

which he passed at Oxford. The final test that came to him, the news that his boy had made the supreme sacrifice on the field of honor in Flanders, he bore with that equanimity which is the crown of a sensitive and unselfish soul,—a soul that lives in God for man, and therefore can never be lost in sorrow nor die in death.

After his own custom, I have been considering what wise and ancient words may best express his personality.

Most of all he would have liked, I am sure, the words of Christ which he quoted to the students of Yale University in 1913: "Ye must be born of the Spirit." That spiritual birth was the secret of the extraordinary power with which Osler used his rare intellectual gifts and scientific attainments.

But next to that quotation from his favorite book, the Bible, I think he would have liked these words written by Tacitus about his father-in-law, the noble Roman Agricola.

"The end of his life brought mourning to us, melancholy to his friends, solicitude even to the bystander and those who knew him not. The great public itself, and this busy, preoccupied city, talked of him in public gatherings and private circles. No one, hearing of his death, was happy or soon forgetful. . . . Should posterity desire to know what

THE HEALING GIFT

he looked like, he was well-proportioned rather than imposing; there was no impatience in his face; its dominant expression was benign. You could easily believe him good, and gladly recognize him great. Though snatched away in his prime, he lived to a ripe old age, measured by renown. He fulfilled the true blessings of life which lie in character. . . . If there be a habitation for the spirits of the just; if, as wise men are happy to believe, the soul that is great perishes not with the body, may you rest in peace, and summon us from weak repinings and womanish tears to the contemplation of those virtues which it were impiety to lament or mourn. Let reverence, and unending thankfulness, and faithful imitation, if our strength permit, be our tribute to your memory. This is true honor: this is the piety of every kindred soul."

XXI

A TRAVELLER FROM ALTRURIA*

THE Dean of American Letters passed away in the spring of 1920, gently and serenely, as he was wont to go in life's affairs. Having lived with a fine faithfulness and joy in labor for more than fourscore years, having finished the last page of his many-leaved manuscript, William Dean Howells laid down his pen, and set out cheerfully on his long voyage to the Undiscovered Country,—shall we not call it his Golden Wedding Journey?

It was sixty years ago that he made his début as an author in *Poems of Two Friends*, written in comradeship with John James Piatt. Then he wrote a campaign *Life of Abraham Lincoln*, and afterward illuminated the ledger of his youthful consulship in Venice with two lovely series of sketches: *Venetian Life* and *Italian Journeys*. In 1871 he published the first of his charming, intimate, fancifully realistic pieces of fiction, *Their Wedding Journey*. After that not a year passed

* Read before the American Academy of Arts and Letters, New York, March 1, 1921.

A TRAVELLER FROM ALTRURIA

without some fruit from his fertile mind: verse, short story, long story, novel, essay, criticism, sketch of travel, or commentary on life.

He was always a painstaking writer; but it was never a pain for him to write. He liked it; and the sense of his own pleasure in finding the right words to describe the people and things that he had in his mind's eye was, (to me at least,) a distinct addition to the pleasure of reading his work. It was perfectly natural for him to be an artist in literature. His feeling of security and comfort in writing clear and beautiful English was at the farthest remove from vanity or priggishness. It was simply the result of keeping good company among books and men. It would have been as unnatural for him to write loud, ungainly things, as for Raphael to paint a Cubist picture.

There was something singularly humane and sympathetic, intelligent and teachable about his spirit. Though of a very quiet manner, he was capable, even after middle age, of strong enthusiasms,—witness his adoration of Tolstoy.

His own careful and almost meticulous taste in words did not prevent him from knowing and understanding the colloquial speech of the day,—

that broad river of so-called "slang" which carries on its flood much perishable rubbish, but also many treasures to enrich the language with new phrases and figures. No doubt the New England School of writers and the stringent intellectual climate of Boston influenced Howells strongly, especially at the beginning of his career. But no less clearly do we recognize in his work the genial influence of the Knickerbocker School, begun by Washington Irving and carried on by George William Curtis, Charles Dudley Warner, Donald Mitchell, Frank Stockton, Henry Bunner, Hopkinson Smith, Brander Matthews, and others. In fact there was in Howells a quality of appreciation and responsiveness which made him open to influences of various kinds, as his book *My Literary Passions* clearly shows.

As a critic, it seems to me, the lasting value of his work is discounted a little by this susceptibility. His criticism is sincere, vivacious, often charming by its very personalism. But it is more a statement of successive likings, than a dispassionate and reasoned judgment. He has no real standard of excellence; or rather, he has too many standards of predilection. Yet it was this very quality that made him so generous and encouraging as a friend to the younger writers of his day, though so far from infallible as a prophet regarding them.

In verse he wrote comparatively little, but in that little he condensed the very essence of his deepest thoughts and emotions. Here we feel that wistful sadness which the true humorist so often carries in his heart: here we can trace the secret furrows which personal grief, (especially the loss of his beloved daughter,) ploughed in his soul: here also we find the humble, hardy blooms of spiritual faith and ethical conviction, surviving all the assaults of sorrow and doubt. He did not lose the will to believe, though sometimes he had to fall back on sheer moral loyalty to defend it. He was an inveterate questioner, an habitual sceptic in the old Greek sense of the word, which means an inquirer, a searcher. But underneath all he was a mystic, unwilling to surrender realities invisible and eternal, or to

"Deny the things past finding out."

Three veins, it seems to me, are clearly marked in his novels and stories. The first vein is a delicate and delightful humor, altogether native, quaint, and savory,—the humor which brings the smile before the laugh. This I find at its best in "A Chance Acquaintance," "A Fearful Responsibility," and that absurdly delightful love-story "The Lady of the Aroostook."

The second vein is a sincere and reasonable realism, an endeavor to be true to the facts of life, material and spiritual. This is quite a different thing from the gross "naturalism," as they call it, of those novelists who are imperfectly house-broken. The stories of Howells are clean, not by force of prudery, but by virtue of decency. I do not know where to find more closely studied, accurately drawn, well-composed pictures, large and small, of real life in certain parts of America at the close of the nineteenth century, than in such novels as *A Modern Instance*, *Dr. Breen's Practice*, and *The Rise of Silas Lapham*. The last in particular, with all its predominant Bostonian atmosphere, is lifted by its moral force into a broader region. It seems to me Howells's best book. I think it comes nearer than any other yet written to that much-called-for but perhaps impossible achievement, "*the* American Novel."

The third vein in Howells's work is the social pas-

A TRAVELLER FROM ALTRURIA

sion, the sense of something shamefully wrong in modern civilization, the intense desire for a new and better life. This, according to his own statement, is directly traceable to what he calls the noblest of his enthusiasms, his "devotion for the writings of Lyof Tolstoy." This came to him, he tells us, just after he had "turned the corner of his fiftieth year,"—that is to say either in 1886 or 1887, according as you take the "corner" as the first or the last of his year. In 1888 he published *Annie Kilburn*, the earliest of his books in which this Tolstoyan influence is unmistakable,—a novel which had such a place in his affection that he sent it to me with his own portrait, as if to say, "Here I am, and thus I believe."

In many volumes which followed,—*A Hazard of New Fortunes*, *A Traveller from Altruria*, *The World of Chance*, *New Leaf Mills*, and so on,— we find the same vein, worked with varying power, but always, if I mistake not, with unvarying sincerity and loyalty to his master's cause. There was, of course, a large elemental force in the Russian master that the disciple did not possess. But on the other hand, the American disciple had a keenness of perception, a balance of judgment, a shrewd common sense that the master had not. You might resume the difference roughly by saying that Howells was a grown-up man of power, while Tolstoy was an infant of genius.

I used to have the impression that Howells's admiration of Tolstoy was unlimited and indiscriminate. I now confess that this was a mistake. It may have been extreme, but it was not without discrimination. Howells admits that his master's doctrine of absolute individualism and passive resistance, like his theory in regard to Money, "though it may be logical, is not reasonable." He discounts the ineffectiveness of Tolstoy's allegories and didactic tales. He faults *The Kreutzer Sonata* for applying to marriage in general the lesson of one evil marriage. He concedes that in certain things the master's life was fallible and seems a failure. And he concludes with a very noble sentence: "There was but one life ever lived upon the earth which was without failure, and that was Christ's, whose erring and stumbling follower Tolstoy is."

As I look back among my personal memories of Howells, which run through more than thirty years, there comes to me somehow a gleam of rare brightness from one unforgettable season.

A TRAVELLER FROM ALTRURIA

We had passed the summer of 1898 as neighbors at York Harbor on the Maine coast. There were others of the guild of letters in the little colony,— Mabie and Warner and Thomas Nelson Page and Kate Douglas Wiggin. We met often, and of course, there was an "authors' reading" for some good local cause to which we all contributed of "such as we had." Yet during the summer each of us was more or less busy with his own task of writing,— Howells more.

But in September came a golden leisure time, when the air was opal with the light sea haze, and hints of autumnal color gleamed secretly through the fading green of grove and thicket, and the marsh-grasses turned russet brown and the bracken dim gold, and the asters put on royal purple, and the long filmy gossamers went floating with the slow breeze or lay on the emerald aftermath glistening with tiny drops like threaded diamonds. Then Howells walked with me in the high pastures, or under the pointed firs, or in the old fields where mushrooms grew for our gathering. The sunset came early but faded slowly. There was a smell of ripening apples and wild grapes. The blue smoke from farmhouse chimneys went straight up into the sky. We could feel that frost was coming,—not far away.

Howells talked with me of nature and art, of books and people, of love and sorrow, of life and death and life beyond. Speaking of his own poetry he called himself "a sadder singer, full of doubt and misgiving." Nothing on earth could be to him what it used to be before his daughter died. Yet he would not give up his work, nor go mourning silent all his days. The best that he would have men say of his writing was that it was true to what he thought and felt when he wrote it. Whatever there was of misery and trouble and evil in the world, still courage and patience, labor and fellowship were good,—good in themselves and good in their results. Justice was what we ought to work for, but meantime most of us must confess that we needed charity,—authors not exempt,—nor preachers! A man ought to think more of what he belongs to, than of what belongs to him. When we see something queer in others it should be a kind of a looking-glass. The best hope we can have is that God smiles at us as we do at our small children. The things we toil for on earth are not vain, —they are real enough, some of them, but all tran-

A TRAVELLER FROM ALTRURIA

sient,—and some day, perhaps, we shall look back at them as not very different from these bundles of mushrooms we have been gathering. "I see," he added, with a whimsical smile, "my bundle is a little larger than yours. But that is only because my handkerchief is bigger. Besides, we are going to divide them equally when we get home."

I still see him with that wistful smile on his lips and around the corners of his eyes, and hear his soft, slightly hesitant voice, as he says good-bye at the door of his cottage.

Clyde Belew